LIFE & TRADITION IN SUFFOLK and NORTH-EAST ESSEX

LIFE & TRADITION in SUFFOLK and NORTH-EAST ESSEX

by Norman Smedley

with a map
19 drawings in text
and 137 photographs

LONDON: J. M. DENT & SONS LTD

First published 1976

Printed in Great Britain by
the Aldine Press, Letchworth, Herts,
for J. M. DENT & SONS LTD
Aldine House, Albemarle Street, London

ISBN 0 460 04221 1

Contents

Photographs

Drawings

'O Memory! Shield me from the world's poor strife;
And give these scenes thine everlasting life!'
                        —Robert Bloomfield (1766–1823)

To Beryl

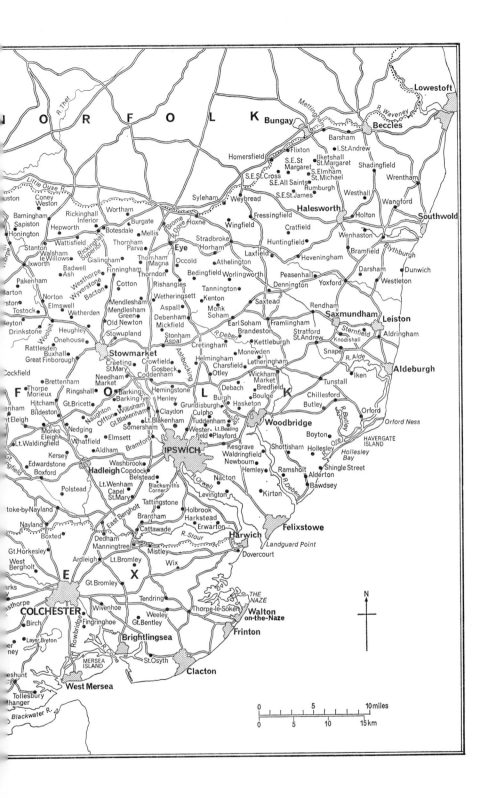

Introduction

It takes a combination of geology, geography and genes to produce a land and its inhabitants. For the beginnings of our area we must go back over a hundred million years, when the abundant life of the Cretaceous Sea was raining down the shelly and plant remains that went to form the Chalk, which attains a depth of some nine hundred feet in parts and makes a major contribution to the composition of the soils that form much of the land surface. As the sea shallowed, sandy beds were laid down followed by clays (the Reading beds), still used in brick making, and producing the blocks of concretionary sandstone known as sarsens, which were later to be fashioned into saddle-querns for the grinding of the corn grown by the folk of the Neolithic period. It was from the discovery of the possibilities inherent in the deliberate planting of seeds to give crops, and the herding of animals, that farming as we know it developed.

The great rivers which followed as the land rose gave us the London Clay, which provided two valuable building materials—it was used in brick making and also gave rise to huge concretions of limestone, the septaria, used as building blocks since Roman times, a use splendidly illustrated in Orford Castle, built by Henry II in 1165–72.

In later periods the animals that roved the scene deposited their faeces which, in their fossilized form as coprolites—phosphatic nodules—gave rise to the first artificial fertilizer industry, established about 1850 in Ipswich by Edward Packard. So, just as until recent years the excrement of farm animals provided the bulk of the manure for our fields, the beasts of some sixty or seventy million years ago began the process which was to supplant natural manure to such a great extent.

As the sea again encroached upon the land, it laid down beds of shelly sand known as the Crag, the earliest of which, the Coralline Crag, was of sufficiently compact form to be used as a building material; Crag was also used as a fertilizer.

The coming of the ice, advancing and retreating alternately over a period of a million years, completed the form of the land surface as we know it, breaking up the underlying formations, and intermingling their components to form the

Boulder Clay which is the essential feature of most of the agricultural land of our region. The vagaries of the ice-flow, with its alternation of intense freezing and interglacial periods, resulted in a variety of soil patterns, with clays, loams and sands not only distributed over the area, but even found in the same field. On the whole, the central area of Suffolk consists of Chalky Boulder Clay, with alkaline sandy soils to the west, directly overlying the Chalk, whilst the east coastal strip, the Sandlings, has an acid character, and has developed into heathland. Peat is found mainly to the north-west, linking with that of Cambridgeshire and the area of North Norfolk round the Wash, but turbaries also existed in the strip which extends almost to Great Yarmouth.*

So the scene is set for Man's occupation. He was certainly here in the Palaeolithic era of food-gathering as distinct from cultivation. One such early culture —the Clactonian—takes its name from the Essex town, whilst at Hoxne, in Suffolk, in a *till* usually regarded as associated with an interglacial period of much the same date, John Frere found worked flints which he recognized as being artefacts. In a paper read before the Society of Antiquaries on 22nd June 1797, he described them as 'fabricated by a people which had not the use of metals' and belonging to 'a very remote period indeed, even beyond that of the present world'. So was initiated the science of Prehistory.

The nearness of East Anglia to the Continent made it a natural target for tribes in search of *Lebensraum*, and pressures due not only to increasing population, but also to displacements from even farther afield, brought wave after wave of invaders to our shores.

The nature of the soil largely governed choice of locality; until the introduction of the heavy plough in Belgic and Roman times, settlement was largely confined to the light lands. Frequent finds of flint implements of the Neolithic and Beaker periods, and the tumuli of the Beaker and Bronze Age (sometimes yielding weapons of bronze), testify to this. At Burgh, in Suffolk, a Roman villa overlying an extensive Belgic (Iron Age) occupation marks the continuation of farming on the same site.

The capture of Caratacus in A.D. 43, and the consequent surrender of Camulodunum, the capital founded by his father, Cunobelin, to Claudius in person, was followed by the establishment of a *colonia* for time-expired troops, and intermarriage must have introduced a strong new element into the local population.

The coming of the Anglo-Saxons, first from what is now the Netherlands, and later from farther north, under leadership derived from the Uppland region of

* For a comprehensive account of Suffolk geology, see H. E. P. Spencer, *Transactions of the Suffolk Naturalists' Society*, vol. 13, pts 4, 5 and 6, 1966/7, and vol. 15, pts 2, 4 and 6, 1970–2.

Sweden with elements from Denmark, left a strong imprint on East Suffolk, where the ruling dynasty was established. Danes and Normans added their quota, and thus we have in East Anglia a breed apart from the rest of the country.

Communications between East Anglia and the west and north still remain far from easy, and even within the region it is impossible to travel from point to point along the coast without detours inland to avoid the estuaries and rivers.

So the nature and topography of the land have to some extent dictated even the quality of its inhabitants, and their manner of gaining a livelihood, and they too have modified its character to adapt it to their needs.

The great variety of its landscape, forest and field and sea, has been the inspiration of its great artists: Gainsborough who idealized it, and Constable who recorded its beauty in his paintings, and its day-to-day life in his letters.* Even the inexorable advance of industrial development, the factories, the roads, the ranks of pylons marching across the countryside, have failed to obliterate entirely its rural peace.

Bloomfield and Crabbe, of the poets, do most to bring the local scene to life; Benjamin Britten has translated it into sound. Thomas Tusser's 'Good Poyntes of Husbandry', doggerel though they may be, are fascinating and indeed not to be ignored in any serious study of farming on the Suffolk and Essex border; he gave good advice on every aspect of life and work on the farm and in the house —but failed abysmally to profit by it himself.

Sea and rivers have provided a gateway for trade with the Continent; Ipswich and Harwich, rivals over the centuries, still flourish, and now Felixstowe bids fair to eclipse both as new roads increase its ability to handle both imports and exports. Once it was a holiday resort, with promenade and pier and pleasure-steamers; the steamers are gone, the pier is amputated to a fraction of its former half-mile, but it still attracts its quota of summer visitors. Sea and rivers fulfil another need; particularly at the weekends, the bright sails of yachts and dinghies enliven the scene.

The fishing industry, centred on Lowestoft since mediaeval times, has no longer the importance that it had before the two wars, but shipbuilding flourishes, and the town caters for summer visitors.

So we may turn for a closer look at the manner in which the physical attributes of the land and its people have influenced the development of both.

Where my information comes from the work of other writers, I trust that I have made this clear, but wherever possible I have taken as my sources personal

* Published at length by the Suffolk Records Society.

reminiscences such as those recorded by Charles and William Freeman of Stowupland in their diaries, account books as that of William Rogers of Ilketshall St
Margaret, farmer, and W. W. Clouting, blacksmith, of Boyton, and receipted
bills accumulated over the years by farmers and housewives. I have also drawn on
conversations, recorded on tape, which I have had with local people in all walks
of life.

In this way, I hope that I have succeeded in clothing the bare bones with warm
living flesh. To read these things as they are recorded, spontaneously, from day
to day, is to enter as fully as possible into the life of the individual concerned, and
to recapture the atmosphere of his personal doings.

So many people have earned my gratitude that it is impossible to name them
all here. Wherever possible I have acknowledged in the text the help which I have
received from craftsmen and others who have allowed me to watch them at work,
and have submitted to interminable sessions with the tape-recorder.

I owe much to Norman Scarfe, without whom I venture to think that this book
would probably not have been written, and who has such a wide acquaintance
with both counties. Mrs Jack Carter has placed at my disposal her great knowledge
of the Suffolk Photographic Survey, which she has recently reorganized, and on
which I have drawn for many of the photographs reproduced; her husband, who
has farmed in Suffolk all his life, and with whom I have been closely associated
in inaugurating the Abbot's Hall Museum of East Anglian Life, has encouraged,
stimulated and helped throughout. A. B. Johnson and the Rev. Philip Wright
have provided a wealth of information.

Without the diaries of the Freeman family it would have been impossible to
give such a living picture of many aspects of Suffolk life, and I am grateful to Miss
Joyce Freeman for making them available for addition to the Museum archives.

I must acknowledge the help given by the staffs of the Essex and Suffolk
Record Offices, and the Suffolk County Library, and especially the willing aid
given by Miss Marjorie Maynard of the Reference Library.

The preparation of the photographs for publication has been the work of
Mr G. F. Cordy, who has helped greatly also in selecting the most suitable for
reproduction. Most of these come from the extensive collection of the Suffolk
Photographic Survey; others I have taken myself, and I am indebted to the following for allowing their work to be included, and in some cases for providing prints.

My thanks are due to the Director of the Victoria and Albert Museum for
providing the photograph for Plate 3; Mr John Tarlton for 31; Mr Brian Palfrey
for 52–55; Mr A. J. Forrest, 45; the *East Anglian Daily Times*, 62; the Abbot's
Hall Museum, 71.

Photographs from the Suffolk Photographic Survey are as follows: 39–42, 45, 49–51, 56–61, 64, 67, 70, 73, 74, 76, 79, 81, 83, 85, 87, 89–95, 97–103, 108–12, 116, 118, 119–21, 123, 124, 126–33, 135–37.

The remaining photographs I took myself, some for the Museum, but most for the purposes of this book.

Mr S. W. Westcott kindly allowed me to use some of the material he had recorded at Westleton.

My successor as Director of the Abbot's Hall Museum, Geoffrey Wilding, has given me every facility to make drawings and take photographs there, and allowed me full access to the library and archives.

Lastly, but by no means least, my wife has helped in every possible way, checking the typescript and photographs, and putting up with many inconveniences. To her, this book is dedicated.

1 Buildings and Building Materials

With the march of time, the process of building depends less and less on local materials, and the form of buildings less on tradition and more on the whim of the architect. Steel girders and concrete blocks have travelled a long way from the natural sources from which they spring, and in themselves have less affinity with the living beings who exploit them than had the living trees from which came the timber of the earlier dwellings, or even the chalk and flints laid down millions of years ago, or the septaria and the clay in which they were embedded. East Anglia lacks quarryable stone, and this was imported only for the major buildings, the castles of the barons and the houses of God.

Until the seventeenth century at least, timber formed the frame of most of the buildings, whether homes or barns; the fact that so many of them are still standing is a tribute to the lasting quality of oak. The timber frame was designed and assembled in the builder's yard, where his tools and stocks of materials were to hand. The members were then marked off at the junctions with Roman numerals, and these give some idea of dating; up to the seventeenth century they were large, and somewhat crudely scratched with a knife; later they were smaller and neatly cut with a sharp chisel. In order to avoid confusion, e.g. between IX and XI, the former was rendered as VIIII; contractions economized in time and space; XV might appear as X̄, XXV as X̄X̄, and so forth. When all was ready the frame was dismantled and removed to the site, where it was quickly re-assembled, often with the aid of willing neighbours.

The infilling for the studwork was usually wattle and daub. A row of holes was drilled in the upper member and a groove cut in the lower. Staves, pointed at the top and cut to a wedge shape at the bottom, were fitted into the holes, and interlaced horizontally with split hazel wands. This surface was then coated with a mixture of clay reinforced with horsehair, cow-dung and sometimes straw, laid on with a clay dauber, a short-handled two-pronged fork with flat tines. The surface was finished with a coat of plaster, in the earlier period leaving the studs exposed; or the filling might be of brick nogging, the bricks inserted obliquely, forming a herringbone pattern.

The exposed beams form an attractive and often regionally characteristic pattern, but wear led to draughts, and in the seventeenth century the outer coating of plaster was often extended to cover the whole surface. Ill-informed restoration has resulted in many cases in the removal of the plaster, under the impression that its application was itself a case of ill-informed restoration! Towards the end of the century the practice was adopted of nailing laths across the studwork and plastering the whole. This expanse of surface in fact provided a 'canvas' for the exercise of the art of pargetting, of which examples, many of outstanding excellence, are to be seen in both counties. White was the predominant colour, but not infrequently in both Suffolk and Essex the juice of the sloe (*Prunus spinosus* L.) was added to give the colour known as Suffolk pink or, in the Stour valley, Constable pink, although it had been in use long before Constable's time.

As early as the latter part of the sixteenth century a cladding of weather-boarding of oak or elm, pegged to the studwork, was adopted for some farm buildings, but it was not until the late eighteenth century, when deal took the place of hardwood, that this form of walling was extended to dwellings, usually the smaller cottages.

Despite the lack of quarryable stone, certain local materials were found to be suitable for building. These were the remarkable concretions known as septaria, formed as the result of little-understood chemical and physical reactions in the London Clay, and seen to advantage in the building of Orford Castle and at the Abbey of St Osyth; flint, both in dressed and pebble form; the chalk from which the flint is derived; and Coralline Crag, a more compact form of Crag than that used as a fertilizer. Norman Scarfe's description (1960) of this last cannot be bettered: 'a delightful, tobacco-coloured, shelly-textured stone, which weathers a rather buff grey in the church towers of Chillesford and Wantisden.'

Clay, so readily available, provides the basic ingredient not only for the making of bricks, but also of clay-lump, formed by mixing in straw with the clay and shaping it into blocks, which are sun-dried. The usual size in Suffolk is 18 inches by 12 inches by 6 inches, but some 'bats' measure $17 \times 9 \times 6$ inches, and for Essex $12 \times 6 \times 6$ inches has been recorded;* the size varied with the need. The external wall of a small farmyard, built entirely of clay-lump, survived a century or more until rain seeped through a small crack, when the whole wall collapsed.

A building peculiar to Suffolk is the 'shroff hut', a cart-lodge or general purposes shelter of unique construction; a flat roof of horizontal beams is supported by

* Ketteridge and Mays, 1972.

uprights of undressed trunks. On this is piled brushwood, over which the thatch is laid direct (Pl. 4).

It is the abundance of timber-framed buildings that links Suffolk with Essex and distinguishes both from Norfolk, which shares with Suffolk a liberal use of flint, both as pebbles and dressed stone, but Essex has its quota. Flushwork, a combination of dressed flint with freestone, shows both to advantage.

Suffolk and north Essex share also a profusion of fine farm buildings; perhaps the distinction here is the great size of some Essex barns. The Wheat and Barley Barns at Cressing Temple, dated by Cecil Hewett as late thirteenth century, and the barn at Coggeshall Grange which, if it is associated with the Abbey, could be even earlier, are outstanding examples.

No other buildings illustrate so well the use which has been made of the varied materials natural to the region as the churches and other ecclesiastical foundations. The church at Lawford, just south of the Stour, exemplifies well the use of septaria, puddingstone (ice-born as an erratic during the Glacial Epoch), flint and brick, mingling with a foundation of freestone. The guest-house of the Abbey at Cogge-shall is of bricks, perhaps the first to be made in the region, dating back to 1190.

Timber is seen at its best in the finely-carved hammerbeam roofs of many of the churches, notably those of Mildenhall and Needham Market (Pl. 11), or the screens of Nayland and Bramfield (Pl. 12). The roof at Mildenhall suffered from the vandalism of Cromwell's troops. When it was examined by the late Munro Cautley, then Diocesan Architect, he found that though some of the tracery had been shattered by the buckshot fired by the soldiery, the wings of the angels were so finely carved that they fluttered as they were struck, and remained comparatively unscathed, though liberally dosed with pellets.

The churches house other treasures, the work of artists and craftsmen. The bench-ends in some churches are outstanding in carving and characterization (Pl. 14). The monuments themselves are historic, even though the history is local. Fine brasses are, infinitely slowly, but inexorably, being worn away by the enthusiastic activities of brass-rubbers. The towers shelter some notable peals of bells; perhaps the fascination they hold is in some measure responsible for the longevity of some of the ringers.*

The profile of many of the houses reveals an earlier date than interior modernization would imply; the steep angle of the roof intended to drain off the thatch remains when slates or tiles have replaced this. Conversely, the interior may disclose early features hidden by the exterior. Edgar's farmhouse, formerly stand-

* As this was being written, there passed away, at the age of ninety-nine, one such dedicated ringer, who continued until the year of his death.

ing in the ecclesiastical parish of Combs, appeared externally to be of seventeenth-century date, but within it was found that arcade posts penetrated the floor of the upper rooms, supporting arch braces with a crown-post. A fourteenth-century date postulated by J. T. Smith* received documentary confirmation as a result of research by Norman Scarfe, and the building, restored to its state as an 'aisled hall' farmhouse, has been re-erected at the Abbot's Hall Museum.

A chance find during an archaeological excavation at Grimstone End, near Ixworth, on a site producing Late Neolithic material, revealed the foundations of a timber-framed house of apparent sixteenth-century date, illustrating a little-known technique. The soil consists of sand and gravel and, evidently for the purpose of increasing stability, the wall-plates had been laid in puddled chalk. It was later found that the practice was known to the local builder. Chalk, especially in the extreme north-west of Suffolk, is used as a building stone in its own right, cut into bricks; Sam Avery, flint-knapper and builder, spoke of its use in Brandon as a backing for all flint walls.

Surface flints in the form of pebbles were extensively used in the building of our churches, our cottages and even our castles; Wingfield Castle is an impressive example; but flint is seen at its best when dressed and associated with freestone as flushwork. Suffolk abounds in it, Essex perhaps rather less so, although it is seen at its finest at St Osyth. Surface flint does not fracture well; flint for dressing must be taken from a depth of some thirty or forty feet, as our Neolithic ancestors found at Grime's Graves.

Bricks for the earlier buildings in this medium were probably made on the site, as those for the Coggeshall Abbey guest house built in 1190, and the oldest house in Suffolk, Little Wenham Hall, c. 1270 (Pl. 27). The great period of building in brick came, however, in the early to middle sixteenth century. The diaper pattern of black bricks in a red groundwork, seen well in Christchurch Mansion, Ipswich, which was built in 1548, is found throughout the region.

Peg tiles were in common use up to the beginning of the eighteenth century, and the Dutch influence which was already making itself felt in architecture was no doubt responsible for the introduction of pantiles, which were made at almost every brickworks in the two counties. The larger size, and the speed with which they can be fitted, made them particularly popular for farm buildings; the black-glazed variety give cover to many cottages as well as barns, especially in the east of the area. Brunskill's (1971) diagram purporting to show the relative occurrence

* J. T. Smith, 'A 14th-century Aisled House, Edgar's Farm, Stowmarket'. *Proceedings of the Suffolk Institute of Archaeology*, vol. XXVII, 1958.

of plain tiles and pantiles throughout the country is certainly inaccurate, implying as it does that pantiles scarcely appear south of the Waveney.

It is a significant fact that, particularly in the sphere of vernacular architecture, the buildings planned and fashioned by the local builder in earlier times are easier on the eye than more recent erections. Perhaps this is in large measure due to the synthetic, and in themselves uninteresting, materials now employed, but some responsibility must rest on the architect, who seems less concerned with the function of the building than with the opportunity to express himself as artist rather than craftsman, and with the exploitation of land and materials for the greatest financial reward. The net result is overcrowding and monotony.

Sanitary arrangements were primitive, consisting of a simple earth-closet, often at the bottom of the garden. Water-closets were introduced into some of the farmhouses in the mid nineteenth century, but for many cottages the old system prevailed for another hundred years or more. The privy of the Alton Mill House, now removed and re-erected with the mill at the Abbot's Hall Museum, must surely be unique. It was a two-seater (by no means uncommon; three and more seats are known), but it was flushed by means of a culvert running from the mill-pool, and continuing to the river.

2 Crafts and Craftsmen

Craftsmanship grew from the need to provide the equipment to carry on daily life. Primitive man used simple tools, and largely made these himself. As life became more complex, three things happened; some men showed special skills, and employed these to fulfil the needs of the community; these craftsmen tended to set up their workshops wherever the demand indicated, and in the rural areas this tended to be in the villages; some crafts were dependent on a ready source of raw materials, and so the potter built his kilns where there was a plentiful supply of the right kind of clay, as did the brick maker, and the flint knapper worked where good flints were ready to hand.

In time, as we have seen, demand led to a degree of mass production; the Goldhanger plough, made by a village blacksmith, was later turned out in greater numbers by a firm which also produced many other requirements of the farmer, even to the wagons and tumbrils which had formerly been fashioned by the wheelwright; the very craftsmen themselves became the founders of large industrial enterprises, as in the case of Robert Ransome, James Smyth and Richard Garrett. What is saddening is that this progress resulted in the loss of the personal qualities of the craftsman, and the satisfaction he derived from carrying out a task from initiation to completion, and substituted a system of piece-work, repetitive to the last degree of boredom, leaving no incentive but the pay packet at the end of the week, and the bitter determination to struggle to the top of the wage ladder.

It was no unusual state of affairs for a village to include half-a-dozen or more crafts within its limited bounds—blacksmith, wheelwright, saddler, cobbler, cooper, carpenter most frequently, although in some cases crafts were confined; the wheelwright often turned his hand and his skill to carpentry, and made coffins as well as carts, and there are many cases of the combination of wheelwright and blacksmith. Crafts very naturally tended to be hereditary, and many cases are found of brothers working together.

[handwritten annotations in top margin]

THE WHEELWRIGHT (Pls 29–42)

The wheelwright is chosen to begin this account of the country craftsmen because of them all he combined within himself the skills and qualities of so many.

The quality of the wheelwright's work depended on a right choice of materials. Careful selection of timber was as essential to success as the skill to fashion it. He would walk the woods and hedgerows, marking down the trees suitable to his purpose, and might purchase them years before they were even to be cut down. When the time came for felling, it was a matter of team work. Once the tree had fallen, the bark was stripped with the aid of barking-irons, barkers or peelers; body irons for the trunk—the 'right wood'—and shorter 'wrong' irons for the branches, the 'wrongs'. A full set of these irons would vary in length from 2 feet or more to a few inches, though the head in each case was little bigger than a half-crown piece.

Dismembered, the timber was then lashed underneath the pole of a timber-jim ('jill' or 'drag'), and transported to the yard. Some drags had four wheels, but that used by H. W. Baldry, the wheelwright of Horham, Suffolk (who combined his craft with that of mine host of the Horham Dragon*), was a two-wheeler, revealing its age by the fact that its wheels were shod with strakes, and not with a hoop.

Next came the task of cutting the logs into suitable sizes. They were manœuvred over the saw-pit by means of purchases, long wooden levers with hook or chain attachment, or a stout hook with a movable ring through which a pole was thrust to give leverage. Terms used by individual wheelwrights vary, and at Horham this hook was called a 'dog', as were also the angled pins by which the logs were secured over the pit. The pit-saw had a long, heavy blade, not cross-cut, but cutting on the downstroke only. The top-sawyer straddled the mouth of the pit, standing on planks, and operated the tiller handle; a box handle screwed on the other end of the saw was used by the pit-man from below. The trenching-saw, a large form of frame-saw, was used in like manner; it has not varied in construction since it was pictured by Jan Weenix (*c.* 1600) in a symbolic drawing in which the Christ Child appears as top-sawyer, with Joseph as pit-man, whilst two angels manipulate the sawn logs.

After sawing, the timber was stored, the logs so arranged as to allow a current of air to pass freely between them. The cut ends were protected by a coating of cow dung, and seasoning might take for anything from four to ten years.

* In Suffolk, the name of the inn is traditionally preceded by the name of the village.

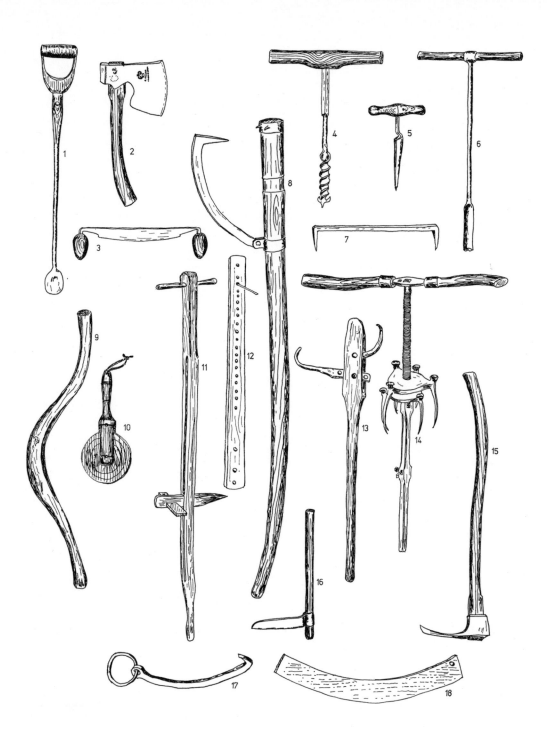

An expert knowledge of the properties of timber is shown in the making of a wheel. Elm, with its twisted grain, was used for the nave or hub, the focal point of the wheel, subjected to stresses and strains from all directions. The spokes must bear the direct weight of the wagon and its load; oak has the strength needed. Resilience is required in the felloes (fellies), the component sections of the rim, and this quality is found in ash, which has so many uses in the making of rural implements.

First the nave was bored out, using the boxing-engine, and the position of the spokes marked off with the compasses. Then the mortises to take the spokes were cut with the auger, and shaped with the bruzz, or mortising chisel. When it was intended to shoe the wheel with strakes, the usual numbers of spokes were ten for the front wheel and twelve for the rear, the tongue of each spoke being squared where it was to fit into the felloe; for hoop tyres the numbers were twelve and fourteen respectively, and the heads of the spokes were rounded.

The dish of the wheel, the degree to which the rim projects beyond the hub, was checked by a gauge consisting of a wooden strip fitted into the hub by a screw, and with a series of holes along its length into which a whalebone strip was fitted, according to the diameter of the wheel.

The wood for the spokes was split to the required thickness by the froe (also called fromard, frower, thrower, river; the name varies from place to place). The blade is set at right angles to the handle, the edge of the blade facing down; it was placed on the timber and struck with a mallet, splitting the log. The spokes were trimmed with the axe, a remarkable implement not intended, like the wood-man's axe, to be swung, but held close up to the head, which has a niche for the finger, and used as a huge knife. The spoke was then smoothed with the draw-knife; the jarvis, used elsewhere to round the outer surface of the spoke, does not seem to have been known to many Suffolk wheelwrights. The length of the spokes was marked off by the trammel, a wooden gauge with a sliding tongue; this does seem to be a local tool, little known in other parts.

As the spokes were driven into the nave, the alignment was corrected by means of the bucker, or type, often a naturally curved branch.

Fig. 1. THE WHEELWRIGHT
1. Barking-iron, bark-peeler. 2. Axe. 3. Draw-shave. 4. Spiral auger. 5. Taper auger. 6. Shell auger. 7. Saw-pit 'dog', holdfast. 8. Purchase (for manipulating timber). 9. Bucker, type, gambrel. 10. Traveller. 11. Trammel. 12. Spoke-set gauge. 13. Spoke-dog. 14. Boxing-engine. 15. Adze. 16. River, froe, fromard, frower, thrower. 17. 'Dog' (used for manœuvring timber, by means of a pole inserted in the ring). 18. Pattern for felloe.
(All figures, $\frac{1}{12}$.)

Ready-cut patterns of different sizes were used to mark out the felloes, and as the latter were fitted on to the spokes, these were strained into position with a spoke-dog or lever-type.

Wagon wheels are 'dished', so that the nave is sunk in a conical depression, with the object of counteracting the stresses resulting from the rock of the wheel on the axle. It also reduces the chances of the rim scraping the body, or of the hub catching a gate-post. It is regulated partly by adjusting the angle at which the spokes are set in the nave, and in part during the process of fitting the tyre, by the degree of pressure exerted by the central screw of the tyring platform. The axle is sloped so that the spokes are vertical as they meet the ground, thus canting out the upper half of the wheel and allowing more room for the body.

When the wheel was finally assembled, the tyre was fitted. If the wheelwright did not combine his craft with that of blacksmith, or was not equipped with a tyring platform, he called on the services of the smith. The latter first measured the outer circumference of the wheel with the traveller, a small wheel of wood or iron, rotating on a short handle. This he ran round the wheel, starting at the junction of two felloes, counting the number of revolutions, and marking off any extra length with chalk. He then took a strip of iron of suitable dimensions, and measured this before cutting it to size. The ends were scarfed or thinned down by hammering, so that the final join would be uniform in thickness. Next the ends were heated and pierced, and the strip placed in a tyre-bender to give it the required curvature. After welding, the whole tyre was heated either over the smithy furnace, being turned to ensure a uniform heat, or by making a circular fire on the ground or, as at the smithy at Belstead in Suffolk, by placing it on edge in a specially constructed upright oven with which that forge is equipped. Meantime, the wheel had been screwed down to the tyring-platform or 'plate'. The hot tyre was placed over it, and rapidly cooled by pouring on cold water to ensure a perfect fit by rapid shrinkage.

The wheelwright of course made not only the wheels but the whole vehicle. When constructing the body, he would chamfer away the wood at the angles of rails and raves and front-boards, and any part of the body where this could be done without loss of strength, in order to reduce the weight. The building of these vehicles, however, belongs rather to the story of transport in general than to that of the wheelwright's craft.

Separate statistics for the number of wheelwrights working in north Essex are not easy to obtain, but those for Suffolk make interesting reading. In 1874 no fewer than 369 are listed; this had dropped to 118 by 1933 and to 98 in 1937. The following years saw the dwindling of the craft, or a changeover to agricultural engineering and other trades. None appears in the Yellow Pages of the current telephone directory, but in fact a few are still working. The corresponding tally for blacksmiths is even more impressive; 503 in 1874, 293 in 1933, 266 in 1937 and 22 at present, although there is still work for farriers.

BLACKSMITH AND FARRIER (Pls 43–4)

No system of classification is infallible, and in no other sphere is this so evident as with the crafts. The links between blacksmith and wheelwright are obvious, and in many cases the two crafts were combined; the blacksmith was not always a farrier, nor the farrier or shoesmith a general smith; often the farrier practised some degree of veterinary service, and the *Key to Farriery*, published by Day, Son and Hewitt, which had run into sixteen editions by 1896, contains no reference to the work of the shoesmith, but is concerned entirely with the treatment of ailments.

The geography of the forge is a model of efficient planning; the furnace, usually of brick, is of sufficient area to take any object for which it is to provide heat, without being unmanageable. Draught is provided by bellows, either standing on the floor to one side, or suspended overhead; these force air through a tuyère, a simple but efficient apparatus, and draught can be varied to give the differing degrees of heat needed for the various operations from mere bending to shaping or welding. In front of the furnace is a cooling trough. The bellows are so placed that the hand can readily be transferred from them to the tools. A simple turn brings the anvil within easy reach.

The anvil stands on a wooden block, usually a section of the trunk of an elm, to raise it to a convenient height. The upper face is of toughened steel; at one end a square tool-hole provides a socket for various implements, and a round punch-hole adjoins it. At the other end the face is stepped down to a small transverse table, of wrought iron or soft steel, on which cutting of iron can be carried out without blunting the chisel. Next comes the rounded and pointed beak ('bick') providing a platform for shaping and bending. Anvil tools are often paired; the bottom swage fits into the tool-hole and has a hollow upper surface into which metal can be beaten to bend it; in combination with the rodded top swage it is used for rounding.

Shoeing calls for a whole range of tools. The old shoe is removed by cutting off the ends of the nails with the buffer, often made from an old rasp. It then comes away easily with the pincers. Next comes the cleaning of the hoof, using the special knife with reflexed tip, and the hoof-parer.

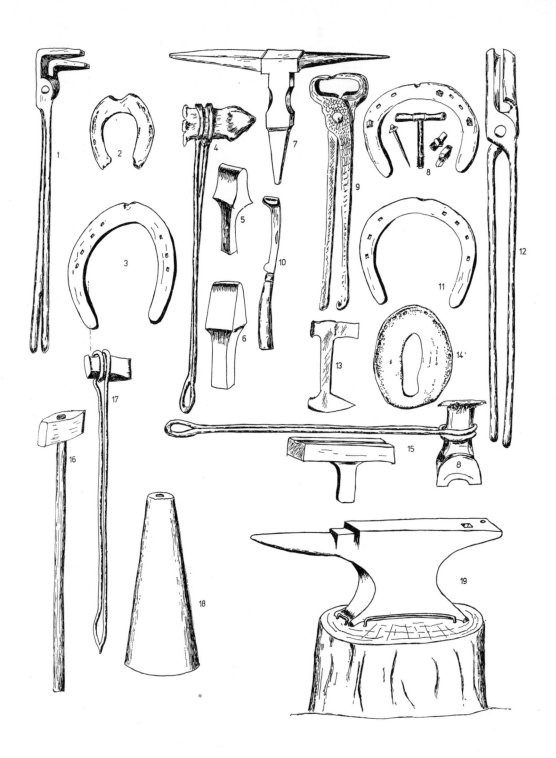

A cold set, a kind of rodded chisel with transverse blade, is used to cut the required length from the bar, by striking it with the sledge-hammer. The catshead hammer is used to beat the bar into shape over the bick of the anvil, and the nail holes are punched with the pritchell. Seating the hot shoe on the hoof causes abundant smoke and an acrid smell of burning, but the hoof is of a horny texture and no pain is incurred.

The popularity of riding and the consequent proliferation of riding schools gives plenty of work for the farrier, and the designing of wrought-iron gates and screens appeals to the younger generation of smiths.

We are fortunate in having had access to the ledgers of the Clouting family, of Boyton, who were smiths there from 1855 until the 1950s, and to the receipted accounts for work done for W. Rogers, of Boundary Farm, Ilketshall St Margaret, by the Shoeing and General Smith in the neighbouring village of Ilketshall St Michael, W. Ford, but much first-hand information has come from Hector Moore of Brandeston, still working and utterly dedicated to his craft. He showed the ledgers of his forbears, who have worked the forge since 1760, and helped to interpret the Boyton ledgers, full of individual idiosyncrasies in spelling. An entry for 28th April 1859 reads:

'Point and put in fork 1 new "furrell" [ferrule]; to Hector Moore, living and working some twenty-five or thirty miles away, it is a "barrel".' Neither word appears in this sense in Moor (1823) or Claxton (1968), and some of the terms used have not been noted by these authors, and are not known to the present generation.

Education in the village school finished at the age of twelve, but the ledgers of the Bradlaugh family (Hector Moore succeeded his maternal grandfather), are written in a copperplate hand which is a matter for envy; the Clouting ledgers show more resort to phonetic spelling. 'Tier' for tyre is understandable; sithe, chissell, handel, sauspan, thumbpeace, stapel and many others are natural renderings with no more significance, and as much justification, as the variations found in Elizabethan manuscripts. On the other hand '1 new "peal spone" [peel spoon] . . . shoeing "tole" [tool]' and 'remaking 10 teeth to coomb', reflect the East

Fig. 2. THE BLACKSMITH
1. Tongs ('duckbill', lipped). 2. Horseshoe, 17th century. 3. Shoe from Suffolk horse (off hindfoot). 4. Punch. 5. Hardy. 6. Fuller. 7. Mandrel (to fit tool-hole of anvil). 8. Horseshoe with frost-nails (3 kinds) and 'tap'. 9. Pincers. 10. Hoof-cleaning knife. 11. Shoe from Suffolk horse (near forefoot). 12. Tongs (hollow-mouthed). 13. Buffer (made from an old rasp). 14. Round-shoe (for damaged foot). 15. Top and bottom (anvil) swages. 16. Hot set. 17. Cold set. 18. Floor mandrel. 19. Anvil. (Nos. 18 and 19, $\frac{1}{12}$; remainder, $\frac{1}{6}$.)

Anglian tendency to transpose 'o' and 'oo'. Where dialect changes the vowel sound this is reproduced in the written word . . . 'two heaters to kittle stand'.

The ledgers are a storehouse of local words, some not even in the dictionaries so far produced, some variants of these. Efforts to find someone who will remember them are not always successful, but the calling of the customer may provide a clue.

Two entries in an account rendered to James Fairhead by William Clouting in 1859 instance this:

'Oct. 4.   6 turndown dorgs 27 lbs. 4½d.   10.   1½
       6.   New dorgs & speakons 4½d. 35 lbs.   13.   1½'

The Fairhead family were wheelwrights in the village of Tunstall, not a far cry from Boyton. Turndown dogs were used to secure the logs over the saw-pit; speakons (spekens in Moor, speakins in Claxton) were large nails, often sold by weight at the time.

Everyone called upon the services of the blacksmith sooner or later. The men who dug the coprolites for use in making fertilizer, 'Mr. Ling, Coperliter' and 'Ealey Sutton, Coproliter' went to Wm. Clouting for '4 shoes to poney', 'hoop iron and nails to barrow', 'iron up siv, new bottom irons', 'altering cart axcel', and 'new handles to sives and fixing'. The innkeeper had a tie and boss for a bulging wall and 'altering water trow irons'. Phillip Spall had '1 new axx' at a cost of 3s., his teapot mended for 2d., and a new ear put on a pail for 3d. Mending a bail and grinding the scythe, referred to the bail used with the scythe for mowing barley, but 'Layd bail & put ears on tub altering hoops' introduced another meaning of the word bail, a handle, and when Hector Moore displayed a splendid example of a horse-breaking bit, with a curved bar to pass under the lower jaw, he said, 'That is a bail'.

W. Shawe, engaged in digging clay for the process of 'claying' the land, took in his beetle for repair, and was charged 1s. 6d. for '2 hoops to beetel' and 8d. for 'stumping beetel'.

The services of the smith were in constant demand for sharpening such items as scythes, hay knives and chaff knives. A frequent entry was 'grind for the year', for which he charged 1s. 0d., not a bad proposition for the farmer, as the charge for grinding one scythe was usually 4d. New tines were made for harrows, and worn hoes and other tools 'laid'—a new piece was added, and the blade reground.

Another entry recurring at intervals was 'Hanging sithe', a somewhat involved operation although the charge made was generally only 3d. or 4d. Hector Moore described the process in detail.

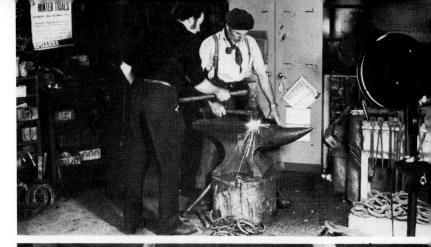

38. *The last strake needs short-ening; the smith holds the hot set whilst his assistant wields the sledge-hammer.*

FITTING *A* HOOPED TYRE ON *A* WHEEL, AT BILDESTON.

39. *Welding a tyre.*

40. *Checking the inner circum-ference with the 'traveller'.*

41. *Placing the hot tyre on the wheel, which is secured to the tyring platform.*

42. *Contracting the tyre by pouring on water to ensure a tight fit.*

The scythe had to be adjusted for the man who was to use it; it was a very individual tool. The 'snead' (handle) was placed against the shoulder, so that the position of the hand-grips (nibs according to Allan Jobson (1953), tacks to Hector Moore) could be determined.

'The first tack was from the tip of the shoulder to the finger-tips, and then the next tack was from your finger-tips to your elbow. When you hang the scythe, you used to lay your first tack on the finger, like that [demonstrating], and the whole scythe would balance, at 45 degrees, sticking out. If that didn't, that wouldn't hang right. They used to swear they'd get sore shoulders if that didn't do that. Yes, that was always "hanging" the scythe.'

Different scythes for different jobs; 'beat out whin sithe' calls to mind that whin, furze or gorse was used, after crushing, as a winter feed, and was also bound into faggots for heating the oven and the kiln. In some areas it was even grown as a crop for the purpose, but on the eastern sandlings it grew, and still grows, in plenty. A new ditch scythe cost 2s. 6d.

Mr Martin, the miller, took his mill-bills to be ground, and Jephther Pottle, mole-catcher, brought his mole spear for repair. The new 'twisseler' bought by John Smith was the scud-winder or throw-crook, used for making straw ropes.

The Rev. G. C. Hoste, the rector, was a good customer; his 'pramulater' seems to have been in constant need of repair; perhaps his 'quiver was full'; perhaps for the same reason his wife's washing-machine and 'ringing' machine had to have attention.

Household utensils brought for the ministrations of the smith included candle-snuffers, a bed-warmer, box-irons and the making of new heaters for these, oven peels and forks, kettles, saucepans, and even the odd mousetrap.

Because of the rough roads of the time, horses had to be shod frequently. In 1820 Charles Freeman had his horses shod every three weeks. For his bay mare, which he rode often, the cost was 2s. 4d., for his dun horse, probably a cart-horse, 1s. 4d. or sometimes 1s. 2d. The charge made by the Clouting family in 1893 was 2s. 4d. for a cart-horse, with an extra 2d. for a riding horse, rising by 1899 by only 2d. In 1899, the basic charge was 2s. 6d., in 1900, 2s. 8d.; 1909, 3s. 0d.; 1917, 4s. 0d. There was a rapid increase after the First World War until in 1921 the charge reached 9s. 0d. A decline followed, to 7s. 0d. in 1922, and 6s. 0d. in 1926. When Hector Moore started work in 1936, the charge for four shoes was 6s. 8d.; it is now £5 + VAT.

Just as the farmers used to contract for the grinding of tools, so did they in some cases for shoeing; 'but that farm over there, I've heard my grandfather say that they'd twelve horses over there and an odd one—what they call a yard horse —that's thirteen horses, and they used to contract to shoe that eleven pound a year, and often they'd want shoeing every ten days.'

'I've shod a horse on a Monday, and again on a Friday.'

Such regular necessary expense called for every possible means of economizing, and a frequent entry is '1 old shoe'. Hector Moore explained this:

'In the case of an old shoe, when the horse has lost one, you go to the scrap heap and pick one up, and tack that on just to get them over till they have the horse shod with four new ones.'

Still more frequent is an item for 'Two shoes, 2 rem.' (removed). In this case, two shoes have been so worn that replacement is imperative; the remaining two are still serviceable, but the foot had 'gone long', so the farrier had to remove them, trim the hoof, and replace them.

A very informative entry is one made in 1922, in an account with B. Poole Esq., Butley Abbey, for

'4 removes layd. heels Entire Horse   6. 9.'

The Entire Horse is of course a stallion. In this case the shoes had to be removed and the hooves pared, but the shoes were also badly worn at the heels, and so had to be 'laid'. A piece of iron of the requisite size was selected for each heel, and this and the heel drawn down, and the two laid one upon the other and welded, thus restoring the shoe to its normal length.

Another process used to counteract excessive wear was steeling. Where a horse was inclined to drag one foot, causing excessive wear at one point, the shoe was removed, and a cut made in the iron. A piece of steel, from a discarded tool, was welded into the gap, giving extra strength. When a horse struck sparks as his shoes came into contact with a stone on the road, steeling was often the cause. A sharp edge could be given to an iron tool in the same way. 'If you wanted a sharp edge on one side, and not in the centre, well, you never split it, you laid the steel on the outside.'

Winter brought the need to take steps to prevent slipping on the icy roads. Frost-nails were driven into the shoes at intervals. Some were small, with pyramidal heads, and were simply substituted for ordinary nails. Others were larger and stouter, and for these some holes, usually three in a shoe, were rived out by means of the 'tap', a die with which the hole was threaded, and the nail was screwed in. As a temporary expedient, a method known as 'roughing' was employed. The shoe was removed, and the clip in the front and the heels were turned down. This was only done when urgent action was called for, and there was no time to frost-nail, or the shoes were so worn that it was better to wait for new shoes before that was done. Roughing and turning-up are synonymous terms.

The farrier was the forerunner of the horse-doctor, and so of the veterinary surgeon:

'1903. Jun. 9. 1 bar shoe. 1 leather sole
     and dressing lame foot   1. 10.'

The bar-shoe, as its name implies, had a bar connecting the heels, and merged by gradations, according to the special needs of each case, into the round-shoe, which is a continuous oval. A leather sole might be added if the foot needed extra protection.

As the need for the farrier's services as horse-doctor grew, he would make the tools needed for the purpose: farrier's gag (horse-gag or balling-iron), ball-gun, tooth-rasp, and the chisel for the removal of a 'wolf-tooth' (see page 110). Recipes for the various ailments to which a horse is subject, and for controlling his moods, were passed down by word of mouth, or written down.

One such MS. booklet in the possession of the Rogers family of Ilketshall St Margaret gives the following:

    To keep the nods of horses
take the Drigs of hartshorne and rub on them.

    To make a horse Draw
put him in a long of Trace chain him to a tree and hit him Inside of his knees with a stick till you Bring him Down then whip him over the wallows till he Draw on his knees then coax him and give him comfort then whip him and serve him so till he Draw kindly.

    To make a horse lie Down
Get some Grey Toads and hang them on the white thorne Bush till they are Dead then Lay them into an ant hill then put them into a small stream take that which separate form the other Dry and Beat them into powder touch the horse on the Pit of the shoulder to Jade him and on the rump to Draw him.

art of catching vicous horses or wild colts in any Place you must Get by the wind and take with you scented cakes made as follows a pound of wheat flower mixed up with treacle made Into four cakes and slack Baked then sweat them under your arm scent them with oil of originum, oil of cinnamon, oil of Fennel and oil of rosemary if you have not time to make cakes you may scent a piece of gingerbread and give him that and it will answer the same purpose.

To manage restive horses or wild colts

To make him stand still to be shod or to prepare them to be sold at a Fair you may numb or stupify them or sleep them give them the Tincture of opium or Laudunum the quantity according to the strength of the horse also $\frac{3}{4}$ oz Digitalis $\frac{1}{4}$ oz Henbane or Black Drops from 25 to 40.

To manage a restive horse so as to be able to Do anything with him Take ten Drops of oil of originum fifteen Drops of oil of cummon oil of penny royal Drop the above oils on one quarter of an ounce of Lunas or orris powder and apply it to the tongue ears or nostril of the horse.

To make a horse cover when he is unwilling

First give him $\frac{1}{2}$ pint west india castor oil to keep his Bowels a few Days Before you want him to cover and a few hours Before going to cover give him as follows two table spoonfuls of Tincture cantharides or 2 table spoonfuls of Tincture Lytee or oil of rape or oil of Terebinth or $\frac{1}{4}$ oz of spirit of nitre or $\frac{1}{4}$ oz Juniper If these should Fail then you may give him one table spoonful of Tincture of Euphorium But this requires Grate care.

Hector Moore was certain, and no doubt rightly, that success in controlling a horse was dependent on the ability to establish a good relation with it, and that this is a quality not possessed by all. He had never had recourse to a horse-stocks such as that at the Belstead forge. He is a firm believer in the old remedies but affirms that it was the practice of the older horse-doctors and horsemen to disclose only the general ingredients of each recipe, at least in the written version, revealing the one essential only by word of mouth. Be this as it may, it is certain that the effective use, particularly of those remedies concerned with control, was the prerogative of the few.

So the blacksmith gave service to all the community; he joined too in its social and religious activities; there are many instances of smiths who were members of the team of bell-ringers, and also organists.

The smithy, too, was not just a place of work; almost equally with the inn it was a meeting place for the local worthies, basking in the glow of the furnace, listening to the clang of iron on iron, savouring the pungent smell of the singed hooves, invoking a nostalgia for the gentle, friendly, peaceful life which has been swept away to give place to an era of petrol fumes, blaring horns and speeding juggernauts.

Hear the smith himself: 'I'm not so happy now as I was getting a half-a-crown a week. They were wonderful old times. We still had a four-and-a-half gallon cask of beer under the bench, but now you can't. Everybody could be wet'—taking out a horn tumbler—'it's still here, look, and that never was washed out!'

Wheelwright and blacksmith; there were many other craftsmen, but none made so great an impact on the way of life of the community; none has left behind so great a vacuum.

THE SADDLER

So long as the horse remained the main source of motive power on the farm and the road, there was work for the saddler, and since the products of his craft, like those of wheelwright and blacksmith, were subject to wear and tear and the need for overhaul, he had a niche in the local economy.

Just as farriers and blacksmiths were to be found in places carrying on their separate avocations, so there was some specialization amongst saddlers, some engaged exclusively in making saddles, some specializing as collar-makers or harness-makers, but this was usually in the market towns. The village saddler was in the main equipped to cater for all local needs, not only for horses both for draught work and riding, but also for supplying belts and straps for man and machine, making weaning collars for the calves, anti-suckling harness for cattle, lawn-boots to prevent damage from the heavy shoes as the horse drew mower or roller, and a great variety of gear entailing the use of leather for its manufacture.

As the pattern changed, and the heavy horse was employed less and less, specialization decreased; the rural saddler was increasingly concerned with riding equipment, his urban counterpart turning to the supply of bags and travelling cases, and even leather coats and articles of household use.

The working gear of the true craftsman has changed little, and many of the tools were passed down from father to son through several generations. It is not the purpose of this book to give a detailed account of each craft, but rather to relate the craftsman to his place in the community; some description of his tools is necessary to achieve this.

One feature of many crafts, but differing in the manner in which it is accomplished, is the devising of a means to control the material whilst freeing the hands for active work. The cobbler has his knee-last, various workers in wood the horse; the saddler employs one of two devices. The clamp, resembling a giant pair of tweezers some 3 ft 6 ins in length, is gripped between the knees so that the leather is firmly held; it is usually of beechwood. The stool, or horse, performs a similar function, and since the jaws are secured by an adjustable latch the craftsman's movements are less restricted.

Of the knives, the most characteristic is that generally known as the 'half-moon', with crescent blade set transversely across the short handle. James Horton of Felixstowe (who was using many of his father's tools) called this the round knife, and its variant with blade set to one side, the half-round knife. Edge-tools, with a grooved blade for bevelling, were 'skivers' to him, though this word is more usually applied to the thinly shaved strips of leather used in delicate work.

Stitching the heavy leather of traces, breechings, collars and the like, requires greater force than the needlework of milliner or dressmaker; the stitch holes are first marked out with a stitch-punch with comb-like head, or with a prick wheel or roulette, with interchangeable head according to the length of stitch. The holes are next pricked with the awl, and the needle forced through with the hand-iron or, in the case of collar-making, the palm-iron which is, as it were, the converse of the thimble, being concave and pitted within; the neck of this instrument is slotted to grip the needle and pull it through on the other side. The collar needle is strongly curved.

The creaser, crease or vein is heated before being used to make the decorative indented line at the edge of a strap. The single vein has a triangular point at an angle to the stem; parallel lines are impressed with the double vein, sometimes adjustable as to width by means of a screw. Narrow strips are cut with the plough, a complicated instrument with a movable blade.

A stuffing-iron, a long rod with a notched tip, is used for ramming the straw into the wale of a collar; as the body of the collar is stuffed it is beaten into shape with the collar-mallet, a delightful object with a head of lignum vitae, strongly resembling the 'wood' used in the game of bowls. The collar is then packed with flock, and the inner side lined with a striped collar flannel. For the saddle, the seat

Fig. 3. THE SADDLER

1. Half-moon knife, round knife. 2. Awl. 3. Half-round knife. 4. Head knife (for cutting holes in straps, etc.). 5. Clamp. 6. Prick wheel, roulette. 7. Hand-iron. 8. Palm-iron. 9, 10. Stitch-punches. 11. Edge-tool. 12. Edge-tool ('skiver'). 13, 14. Punches. 15. Marker, crease. 16. Vein, crease, creaser. 17, 18. Collar stuffing-irons. 19. Seat iron. 20. Collar-mallet. 21. Horse or stool. (Nos. 5 and 21, $\frac{1}{12}$; remainder, $\frac{1}{3}$.)

iron, a handled rod with flexible tip to avoid damage to the leather, is used in the stuffing process.

Punches of varying shapes and sizes are needed for the making of holes, and to secure rivets.

The leather used by the saddler had first to be tanned, and then treated by the currier to make it flexible; latterly this process also was carried out by the tanner, but in former days many of the small towns and even villages numbered curriers amongst their inhabitants. In some cases the shoe maker was also a currier; he too needed treated leather for his work.

In Suffolk in 1844 there were some 140 saddlers, many of them classified in the directories as 'Collar and Harness Makers', and fewer than 40 curriers. By 1904 the numbers were respectively 154 and 12; in 1922, 110 and 8; in 1937 no curriers are listed as such, but the tanners are classified as 'Tanners and Curriers'. In 1844 Debenham, a town of 1,215 inhabitants, had two curriers and three saddlers.

Leonard Aldous started work with the Debenham saddler, Lionel Rumsey, in 1913, when he was twelve and a half, and about fifteen years later took over the business, retiring and handing over to his nephew in 1967. Between 1837 and 1967 only three names had been associated with this shop: Charles Fulcher, and later his son Thomas; Lionel Rumsey, who worked from the early 1880s to 1928, and Mr Aldous himself. From what he himself told me, and the order book of Charles Fulcher, it is possible to get a very full idea of the work of the village saddler at a time when his services were indispensable to the local community.

The order book gives details, with measurements, of sets of cart and plough harness and other equipment for the farmer—a cow's muzzle supplied in 1842, a stallion bridle in 1855, a bullock's tye, and several separate pieces for both cart- and carriage-horses. An additional interest is provided by the fact that the names of the horses are given in many instances; it was just as necessary for a collar to fit as a set of shoes. Collars for the horses of Mr J. Clarke, of Kenton, supplied in 1840, are listed: Doughty 20 by 10; Procktor 21 by 10; Punch 19 by 9; Depper 20 by 9½. Another Doughty belonging to Mr S. Darby of Aspall needed a collar 20 deep by 9 wide, and Mr Mayhew's Bragg took a measurement of 22 deep by 9½ wide.

Charles Fulcher made neat drawings, with notes to aid him; one of these is labelled, 'A Cavesson or Martingale which you Please'. His thorough methods are illustrated by a page from his book:

	feet	inches
1843. Mr. Wade's Pony's Harness		
May 20. Dutfin Head	—	18

Throat Latch	—	16
Front Clear	—	$10\frac{1}{2}$
Sides 3 loops		7
Nose Pice		24
Billetts		12
Winker Straps		$9\frac{1}{2}$
Drafts	4	4
Girt from Terrett	2	6
Crupper		20
Splitt up		$7\frac{1}{2}$
Billett	2	10
Back and Belly Band	6	9

During Leonard Aldous's working life he had had an even wider range of work than that indicated in Charles Fulcher's record, but the greatest demand was for farm harness, of which collar-making calls for special skill. Rye straw was invariably used for stuffing the wale of the collar.

'We had great difficulty in buying rye straw, and the old person at the shop, when I was a young man there—he had a farm; he farmed about sixty or seventy acres, and he used to set aside a patch, every year or two, and grow with rye straw—not for the corn; before the corn was actually ripe this was cut, so the straw was slightly green, and he used to supply one or two other people with a few bundles of this, and if the land was manured very well, so the corn was long, it was very fine sown, and there were no very large knots in this straw, like there are in wheat straw.'

Later, when Mr Aldous had the business, and had no farm, he had on occasion to use wheat straw. A local farmer would tell him when he had some very good straw, and he and his nephew would go up at about half-past five or six in the morning, when threshing was taking place, and they would pull the straw out of the stack and bind it up. 'Sometimes the farmer would send it home for us' . . . 'Wheat straw was all right for repairs'.

The Debenham saddlers did not as a rule make trap harness, but maintained a stock of sedge collars, and the owner of a cob or pony in need of a new collar would take a sedge collar and use it for three, four or even six months. By the time that it began to show signs of wear it had modelled itself to the shape of the horse's shoulder. It was then taken back to be covered with leather. A sedge collar was worn by a colt whilst it was being broken in, and would be covered at the same time as a set of harness was made. So the farmer would have 'a new set of harness, with the collar already used, and probably the trap all cleaned up, painted, varnished, all ready to use, ready to hook'.

Harry Loveday Ulph, of Chelmsford, now in his eighties, had been faced with a variety of tasks in his time, including making a set of boots for a circus elephant, so that it might travel from place to place on foot. Only recently he produced a set of cob harness, entirely hand-stitched, and presented it to the Abbot's Hall Museum.

THE COBBLER

In the early directories nearly every village is shown as having two or more shoemakers; hand-made boots were the rule rather than the exception.

This was yet another craft in which the free use of the hands was of importance, and the knee-last, a stout pole held between the knees in the same manner as the saddler's clamp, was provided with a number of interchangeable heads for all sizes. A stool was also used, giving a flat surface for working, and a series of partitions for the different sizes of nails.

Before use, the leather from the tannery had to be softened by currying. It was soaked and brushed, the remains of the tanning fluid being forced out by pressure from specially shaped knives, rolled and made pliable by pulling backwards and forwards over a stake. At the same time it was impregnated with a mixture of tallow and cod-liver oil.

Selection of different portions of the skin for different areas of the boot was necessary, to ensure that not only was the strongest and stoutest leather used for the parts most liable to heavy wear, but also that the two boots of a pair were evenly matched.

Fig. 4. THE COBBLER AND THE OSIER-BASKET MAKER
Cobbler
1. Glazer. 2. Double-iron. 3. Waist-iron. 4. Drag-knife. 5. Lasting pincers. 6. Stretching pliers. 7. Knee-last, hobbing-foot. 8. Cobbler's stool. 9. Last-hook. 10. Slide box-wheel. 11. Burnisher. 12. Stitch-pricker. 13. Rasp.

Osier-basket maker
14. Shears. 15. Shell-bodkin, cane-pinker. 16. Pinking-knife. 17. Cleaver. 18. Shave. 19. Cane-rive. 20. Grease-hole. 21. Brake, willow-stripper. 22. Shop-iron. 23. Bodkin. 24. Bundler. 25. Commander.
(Nos. 2, $\frac{1}{6}$; 3, 5 and 7, $\frac{1}{12}$; remainder, $\frac{1}{3}$.)

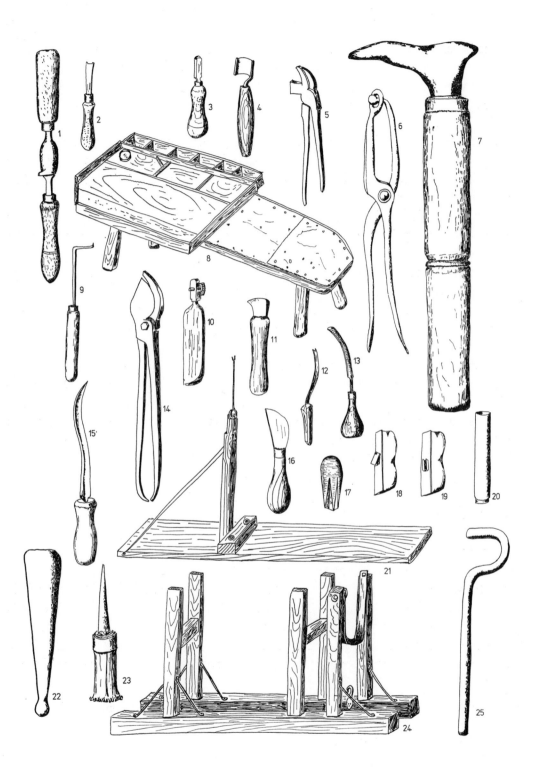

Characteristic tools are the clicking-knife, with slender, slightly curved blade for cutting out the leather for the uppers, and the awls, not handled, but pointed at both ends. That for preparing the insole for stitching on the welt has one end curved, and earned the name in East Anglia of the 'avocet', from its resemblance to the beak of that bird. The lasting pincers drew the leather taut over the last.

The heavy boots worn by the farm-worker, called in Suffolk and Essex 'high-lows', were studded with large nails, and the heels plated. They were worn by young and old alike, and how the lads would joy to strike sparks from the flint of the roads!

Accounts paid by William Rogers to F. Smith of Rumburgh in 1898 and 1901 refer to making 'your new Strong fencers'; the identity of these is lost in the mists of the past, but they may have been the leather oversleeves used for protection when cutting hedges ('fences' in Suffolk). A recent practice is to cut off the tops of an old pair of Wellington boots for this use.

Another account, from S. Bird in 1909, refers to highlows as 'hillows', and includes 'rip lace boots' for the farmer's son and daughter, at 7s. 6d. and 9s. 6d. respectively.

Ninety years earlier, in the 1820s, Charles Freeman was paying 10s. 6d. for a pair of new shoes, 2s. 6d. for a pair of buskins, and 11s. 0d. for the tanning of a horse-skin, presumably for use in repairs which could be carried out on the farm, perhaps the renewal of the leathers on cart shafts and the like; 'mending Boy Ablitt's high-shoes' most probably refers to the knee-boots worn by some house servants, and not to highlows.

THE RAKE MAKER

By contrast with the large numbers of such craftsmen as smiths, cobblers, saddlers and others who supplied the tools and equipment of the farm workers, rake makers were few in number, but their field of distribution was wide. Haughley, in Suffolk, was one such centre, where work was carried out over a period of almost exactly a hundred years, supplying a region covering the whole of East Anglia, and later spreading to include Bedfordshire, Huntingdonshire and parts of Buckingham-shire. The following is based partly on a paper published in June 1956 in *Gwerin*,

Fig. 5. THE RAKE MAKER
1. Draw-knife. 2. Stail-engine. 3. Driving-stool. 4. Bench-anvil. 5. Stock-knife. 6. Hand-anvil. 7. Shaving-horse. 8. Draw-shave.
(Nos. 3, 5 and 7, $\frac{1}{12}$; remainder, $\frac{1}{6}$.)

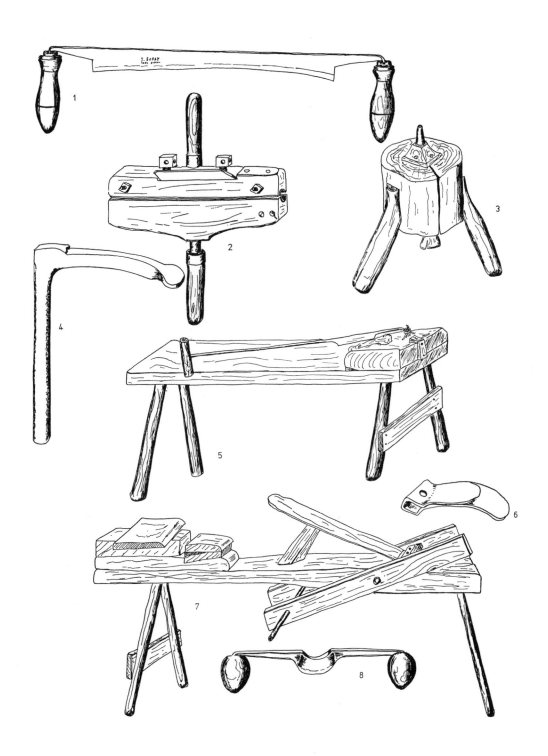

vol. 1, No. 2, by Thomas Bagshawe, and in part on information gleaned locally, after the tools had been deposited in the Abbot's Hall Museum.

Samuel Rye, born in 1800, set up business as a rake and scythe-stick maker in 1853, in three rooms of a timber-framed cottage in Duke Street, Haughley. Ten years later, the business was taken over by his son-in-law (a by no means rare occurrence in Suffolk). Alfred Woods was also the village postmaster, and had worked as a coach-builder. Thomas Cutting left school at the age of twelve in 1903, and went to work for Woods as a telegraph boy at the Post Office, helping on occasion in the workshop and gaining a knowledge of the craft, although with no formal deed of apprenticeship.

Samuel Rye had a flourishing business employing five men, and trade continued to thrive during the first years of Wood's time, but as machinery rendered the use of the rake, scythe and other implements less necessary, trade dwindled, and when Cutting took control in 1932 he employed only one man, at first on full time, then part time; after the Second World War he was working alone.

Although the making of rakes and of the sneads (sticks) and tacks (hand-grips) for scythes was the principal occupation, many other items were produced. Bagshawe quotes the following from the day-book of Samuel Rye:

Hand hay rake with straight handle or stick entering the head (hade, haede) in one place.

Crotch rake (more familiarly, hobby rake or moggy rake), in which the stick is split, entering the head at two points.

Nail rakes or iron rakes, with nails for tines or blacksmith-made iron teeth. (Hobby rakes may have tines of either iron or wood.)

Bow rakes for garden use (usually called daisy rakes).

Seed or sucklen (clover) rakes.

Thaten (thatching) rakes.

The scythe-cradle, to collect the corn as it is cut, was called by Rye a suather, suther, swath, swather, sweather, sweth, swether or swetar rake, or a swet.

Bails, or bales, attached to a scythe when mowing barley, were also made by the rake maker, though they might as often be cut from the hedge by the mower.

Of the various handles, he gives howe sticks (hoes); handles for spades, scud-winders, set-sticks, shackles (attached by a chain or rope to a heavy block of wood to prevent a horse from straying); flails (thraile or thrile) and their component parts, e.g. hand-staff (handstarfe, harnstarfe) and swingel. Then there were fork stales, beetle (beatell) handles; shepherds' crook staffs (crook sticks or shuphard sticks); muck crome handles; turnip crome sticks; plowe sticks; repe hooks; syckels; corn and mud scuppits (cupets); spud sticks; bushel strikes, for levelling off the grain in a bushel measure; whippletrees (wipltres, wipltreses); pitchfork sticks (shake fork, but more usually in Suffolk shoof fork); tat or tap sticks, the screwed wooden taps for the spigot of a barrel.

Ash was most common for the making of handles, but birch, willow, alder and hazel are also found.

Tools are simple but effective. The shaving-horse again provides an efficient means of securing the material whilst leaving the hands free, the feet providing the pressure necessary to grip the stail whilst it is being stripped of its bark (using a peeler identical with that of the wheelwright), or whilst shaving it down with the draw-knife.

The stail is rounded with the stail-engine, a heavy rotary plane. Ash was the usual material for the stail, willow for the head and the tines. These were formed by sawing off short lengths of wood, which were driven through the driving-stool, to all intents and purposes a plane with a circular blade, to round them.

Next, the tines were driven into the head and sharpened with the stock-knife, or tooth-stool, much the same implement as that used by the clog maker for shaping the wooden soles.

Smoothing of the stails was completed by the use of the draw-shave, a draw-knife with rounded blade. Mr Cutting developed a turning machine driven by an engine, for use in conjunction with the stail-engine, and also a treadle-lathe for some handles. Rough home-made implements, a bending-horse for rake stails and a press to which scythe sneads were lashed to give the necessary degree of curve, completed the equipment of the workshop. For smoothing, shagreen was used; sandpaper was too costly.

Arthur Cutting retired in 1952, and the shop was closed; fortunately the tools illustrated joined the collections at the Abbot's Hall Museum.

THE THATCHER (Pls 45–7)

From time immemorial, man has made use of the natural vegetation around him to build himself a home, and to provide it with a roof to keep out the elements; thatching, in one form or another, is as old as man himself.

The numbers of thatchers in Suffolk are not readily available for the earlier years; classified lists do not appear in the directories until the latter part of the nineteenth century, but these figures are of some interest, reflecting as they do some of the changes which have taken place in agricultural methods, and in the use of building materials.

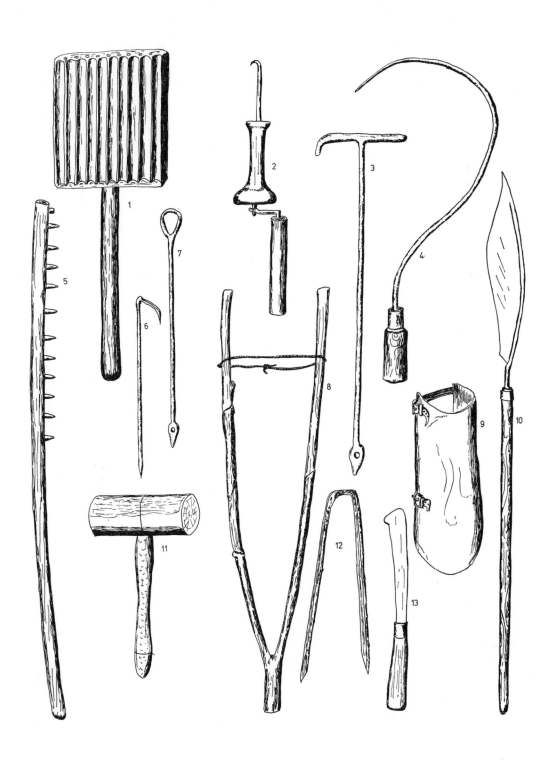

In 1874, 100 thatchers were working in the county; in 1885, 128; in 1892, 134; by 1912, the numbers had declined to 70, and to 31 in 1937.

Up to the end of the seventeenth century the great majority of houses were timber-framed, with thatched roofs, and even after the use of bricks became common, these earlier homes retained their thatch, the need for periodic replacement providing work for the thatcher. This applied in even greater measure to barns and other outbuildings, for even when a change to tiles was made for the house, the barn often kept its thatch.

Stacks were thatched for protection, and although this work was sometimes carried out by the farmer and his men, craftsmen were often called upon for work on the larger farms. In 1822 Charles Freeman paid 12s. 0d. to John Keiry, thatcher, for repairing stacks, and members of the Linnett family, who have been thatchers for some three hundred years, first at Broomfield in Essex and later at East Hanningfield, and latterly at Hawkedon in Suffolk, show records in their day-books of stack thatching in both counties, dating back to the father and grand-father of the present representative of the family, Frank Linnett.

The development of modern harvesting machinery, and the decline of the horse on the farm, have lessened the need to conserve straw; there is no longer any call for the thatching of stacks, or very little; a tarpaulin, or more recently a polythene sheet, serves the purpose. Another effect is the quality of the straw left by the combine harvester; it is too short for thatching, and is crushed as it passes through the machine.

When wheat straw is required for the work, the thatcher will arrange with a farmer to grow a suitable variety, which they themselves will cut with a binder, and thrash with a drum. If straw reed thatching is intended, a special fitment on the drum combs the straw so that all the ears are facing in the same direction. Some local farmers themselves grow, cut and thresh the wheat, selling the straw to the thatchers. In either case, the process is now a costly one; where wheat straw was at one time the common material, Norfolk reed is now more widely used. Much of it comes from the Ranworth Broad in Norfolk, but some is grown in Suffolk. Rye straw is also used; 'it's good and soft', according to Frank Linnett.

It might be expected that the craft would be steadily dying out; on the contrary, it is at present flourishing. Thatched cottages are popular with those who can

Fig. 6. THE THATCHER
1. Leggatt. 2. Scud-winder, throw-crook. 3. Needle. 4. Straw-buncher. 5. Rake. 6. Thatch-hook, thatch-pin. 7. Needle. 8. Yoke. 9. Knee-pad. 10. Eaves-knife. 11. Mallet. 12. Broach. 13. Riving-hook.
(Nos. 5, 8 and 10, $\frac{1}{12}$; remainder, $\frac{1}{6}$.)

afford the luxury of a second home to which they can escape at weekends and holidays; they can usually afford to meet the expense of thatching, and many a cottage which had fallen into a derelict state has been restored to its former charm.

Materials and tools differ only in minor detail in different parts of the country, though the names vary. The straw, which must be of the long-stalked variety, is prepared and used in two different ways. When threshed in the drum in the usual way, it is suitable for long-straw work, in which it is not beaten in with the leggatt, but combed down so that the final effect is of a continuous smooth surface, with a marginal pattern of liggers at the eaves and barges (gable ends).

In reed-thatching, whether Norfolk reed or straw-reed, the yealms or bundles are placed in overlapping courses and secured by liggers or sways, which are fixed to the rafters by thatch-pins, the cut edges presenting a bristly surface; they are levelled by beating with the leggatt, and trimmed with the knife. In Suffolk and Essex straw is always used for the ridges; reed is not sufficiently pliable. Broaches are driven in to hold down the cross-pieces and liggers, and the trimming of the ridges lends itself to distinctive patterns.

The yealms are carried up to the roof in the yoke, preferably a naturally forked branch; if this is not to hand, two branches are joined by means of a triangular wooden block. The straw is collected together with the straw-buncher, a hook with a blade of round section. On the roof, the yealms are supported on a small platform, the reed-holder, which hooks into the thatch.

Needles serve two purposes; they are inserted to hold the thatch in position temporarily until it can be fixed with sways and pins, and are also used for passing the tarred twine through when the thatch is to be tied to the rafters. When this method is employed, the twine is first tied to the ligger then threaded to the needle, which is pushed through to an assistant inside the roof; he passes it round the rafter and sends it up on the other side, where it is once more tied to the ligger.

In the yard behind the thatcher's house are stacked quantities of hazel rods, the raw material for liggers, sways and broaches. All these spars were at one time made by the hurdle maker or other craftsman in wood, and sold to the thatcher, and Frank Linnett may have to resort to this source of supply if stocks run short. He prefers, however, to make his own; he can then regulate the length. For the purpose he uses a riving-hook (spar-hook). Neatly stacked and ready for use are literally thousands of broaches, the fruits of winter days and wet weather. Before the broach is inserted, it is given a sharp twist of the hands in opposite directions, converting it into a staple, and is driven in with a beechwood mallet; a hammer is of course needed for the iron thatch-pin.

Rakes vary from a primitive form made by driving a row of 4-inch nails into a rough wooden handle, to a finely-fashioned rake over 5 feet in length, of ash, with tines of hazel.

The leggatt, for driving in the thatch to give a level surface, has a rectangular flat head on a short handle, with a series of parallel grooves and ridges; for reed the surface is studded with large-headed nails.

To give a final trim to the eaves a long-handled knife, the eaves-knife, is used; formerly it might be made from a discarded scythe blade.

The scud-winder or throw-crook is used for the making of straw rope. Frank Linnett's father used this rope for tying up bundles of hay, but it was often made to hold down stack thatch by means of weights, or to tie up the yealms.

The thatch-pins are often the product of the blacksmith, but Frank Linnett showed with justifiable pride his own small forge, complete with bellows, anvil and bench with vice. Here he makes his own pins.

The day-books of his grandfather, Charles Linnett, and his father, Harry, give some idea of the tremendous rise in cost of thatching in comparatively recent years. In 1828 Charles Freeman recorded a payment to Abbott, thatcher, of Earl Stonham, of £3 for 60 squares of thatching at 1s. 8d. In 1948, a stack was thatched at a cost of 6s. 6d. a square (1 sq. yd.), and in the same year, a cottage was measured up for thatching at 16 yards by 6½ yards, and an estimate given at 4s. 6d. a square. With the cost of materials the final bill was approximately £50. Today, it would cost between £700 and £800. Thatching a hay stack was much less expensive than the work on a corn stack: 1s. 6d. per square.

The durability of thatch varies of course with the quality of the material and the conditions to which it is exposed. Good Norfolk reed is generally given a life of sixty years or so; straw was less durable. However, some idea may be gained from Frank Linnett's recent experience: 'Last year I thatched a house . . . that was the old Post Office, Denston Green. Well, I helped my father to thatch that before I left school.' That would be approximately forty-five years ago. 'He thatched it with straw; he never used to use Norfolk reed, because there was plenty of straw in those days.'

An interesting note on the thatching of stacks appears in *The British Farmers Cyclopaedia* (1808), especially concerning the use of straw ropes:

'When long straw is made use of, the thatcher usually begins at the eaves, depositing it in regular courses or breadths until he reaches the top; the different courses being always so placed as to overlap each other, the upper ends being constantly pushed a little into the sheaves. In this manner he gradually proceeds, course after course, till the whole of the roof of the stack is finished. And in order to confine the thatch in its place, straw ropes are laid along the top and eaves, being pinned down with pointed sticks'.

The objection on the grounds of cost is overruled by suggesting that when removed 'it serves very well as litter for the cart horses and other cattle'.

THE OSIER-BASKET MAKER (Pls 48–9)

Basket making falls into the category of those crafts which are not an essential element in the local economy, but take advantage of local conditions to produce commodities with a distribution extending far outside the immediate area, though in 1874 there was enough demand to keep over forty basket makers busy in Suffolk. Their siting was necessarily influenced by the need for proximity to a river, for they grew their own willows.

Robert Mullins is one of a long line of craftsmen, deriving from two brothers, Thomas and George, who hailed originally from Devizes in Wiltshire. It would appear that George, or one of his progeny, saw the possibilities of Onehouse, a small village on the banks of the River Gipping, and opened up there some time in the nineteenth century. From that time it was the practice for the father to see to the London base of the business, whilst the eldest son attended to the growing of the osiers and the manufacture of the baskets at Onehouse. The requirements of the local farmers and fruit-growers were met; the large basket known as a chaff-basket or winnowing basket was made here. Much of the output, however, went to London; in fact, Mr Mullins stated that it might be said that every basket that went into Smithfield Market was supplied by the firm. Other products were the huge baskets once used by commercial travellers to transport their wares; a traveller would arrive at the draper's shop accompanied by a lad pushing a hand-cart on which rested one or more of these. Then there were the fish-baskets in use before the last war; the flat type used by the fish-merchants, not the crans in which the fish were landed; these were specially made locally. Portmanteaux were another line, and great-grandfather Mullins made a suite of furniture; chairs of basketwork and tables were often made at that time.

Another branch of the family settled at Wickham Market, where the firm is still in being. Photographs are shown of Mr T. T. Mullins at work.

At Onehouse, 100 acres of osier beds were cultivated. When a bed was worked out, it would be cleared and put down to potatoes or some similar crop for the next three years to clean it; 95 acres were therefore in production at any one time.

The willows were cut individually with a hook, using an upward stroke, as near to the ground as possible; by this means soaking of the remaining stool and the danger of rot were avoided. 'We always cut as close as possible—if you give it, like, a head, without any bumps on at all, you get the perfect willow.'

Three methods of preparation, to produce brown, buff or white willow, were used. Describing them, Mr Mullins said: 'The brown is dried without being peeled; the buff is boiled and then peeled; the white is stood out and it grows again, then peeled.' Peeling was carried out by the use of the willow-stripper or brake, an iron fork through which the willow is drawn. Sometimes several of these are set on a stand, side by side; the work was often done by women. Shortly before the war, in the 1930s, a revolving drum with rows of forks was introduced; this speeded up the process, but the results were less satisfactory.

Full details of the process of basket making would take up too much space for inclusion here, but illustrations are given of some of the tools (see Fig. 4).

THE COOPER (Pls 51–4)

To an even greater extent than the basket maker, the cooper was outside the village community, travelling and serving an area. The exception to this was employment within a specific industry, such as the brewery. For the last twenty-three years Brian Palfrey has been cooper to a Suffolk brewery, succeeding his father who served for over half a century in that capacity, and to whom he himself was apprenticed. Nevertheless, he used precisely the same tools and methods as the travelling cooper.

The cooper made a wide variety of containers; casks for home-brewed beer, the small harvest barrels, the tubs and keelers used for the brew and for dairying were his work, as were the wooden pails for milking and carrying water, and even the tubs used by the fishermen at the fishing ports.

In doing this, he used an amazing variety of tools, perhaps more than any craftsman other than the wheelwright. Indeed, although the products of these two craftsmen differ in form and scale, they are akin in their ability to use seemingly crude tools with the utmost delicacy and skill. As the wheelwright's manipulation of his heavy axe is a marvel and a joy to behold, so is the fashioning of the staves of a cask using the cooper's broad-axe. The jointer-plane, with a length of anything up to 6 feet, obviously cannot be used in the ordinary way of planes; it is mounted upside down on a stand, and the staves are drawn across the blade to give them the bevel necessary for a close fit.

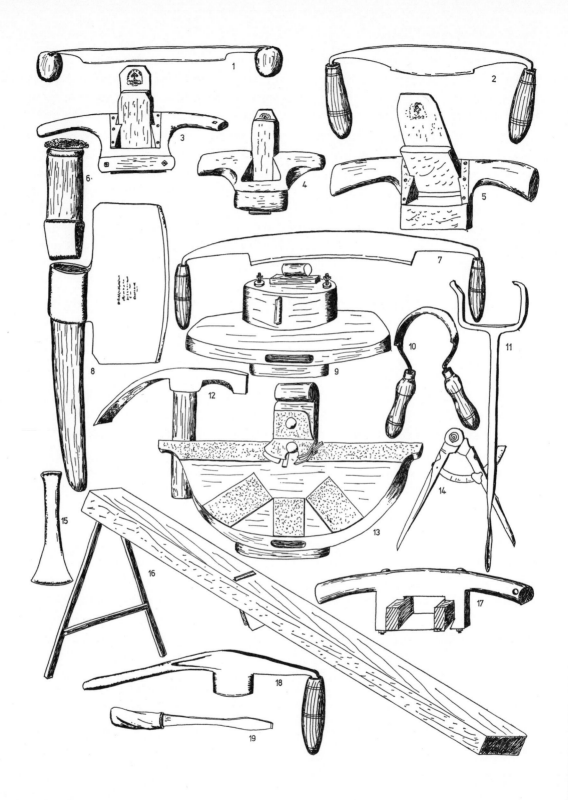

Such an?

The process of making a cask has been well described elsewhere,* and there is no need to give a detailed account here, but some differences in method and tools used by the Suffolk cooper from those elsewhere are of interest, perhaps the more so in view of the close similarity of the process in general.

The shaving-horse was little used, except for the making of wooden pails or small casks. Trussing up was carried out in the normal manner, assembling the staves in an iron raising-hoop and securing them with a truss-hoop of ash; this last was not made by the cooper. The staves were steamed by wetting and suspending the cask over a cresset, in which a fire of shavings and other oddments was lit; they were then drawn together at the top by means of smaller wooden truss-hoops. The adze, with strongly curved blade and short handle, was used to trim the top of the cask to form the chime, and the top was levelled with the sun-plane, with stock curved to travel round the perimeter. Then the jigger, a curved implement akin to a draw-knife, but with one wooden handle and a steel grip at the other end of the blade, smoothed off the interior before the chiv (chive) was used to cut a semicircular groove, the howel, a little way below the chime. The groove to take the head of the cask was cut into the howel by means of the croze.

The apparently arbitrary, but evidently satisfactory, method of calculation of the radius of the head, by stepping the compass round the top until $\frac{1}{6}$ of the circumference is found, seems to be universal, as are the other tools used in making and fitting the head, and beating the hoops into place. The bung is bored with the taper-auger, but the thief, used elsewhere for tidying up the edges of the hole, is unknown here.

OTHER CRAFTS AND INDUSTRIES

The crafts so far described have all, in greater or lesser degree, been factors in establishing the character of our region. It is not possible to treat in such detail the other crafts which have emerged to meet local needs, or to take advantage of

* Jenkins, 1965.

Fig. 7. THE COOPER
1. Draw-knife. 2. Hollowing-knife. 3. Downright-shave. 4. Inside-shave. 5. Heading-swift. 6. Driver. 7. Heading-knife. 8. Broad-axe. 9. Chiv, chive. 10. Two-handed shave. 11. Flagging-iron. 12. Rending-adze. 13. Croze. 14. Compasses. 15. Chintzing-iron. 16. Jointer-plane. 17. Buzz. 18. Jigger. 19. Screwdriver.
(No. 16, $\frac{1}{12}$; remainder, $\frac{1}{6}$.)

local conditions to further their own development. Nevertheless, the picture would be incomplete without some mention of them.

Flint Knapping (Pls 67–8). Two factors have been mainly responsible for the development of this industry; the discovery, as far back as the Neolithic period, of the suitability of flint for the fashioning of tools and weapons; its availability in the Brandon area; and the realization that mining was necessary to obtain the right grade. The other factor was the need to find a suitable material as a substitute for the workable stone lacking in the region. The flint knappers profited from the experience of their early ancestors.

Brick Making (Pls 55–7). Supplies of suitable clay were ready to hand, and hand-made bricks were evidently made in Essex and Suffolk long before they appeared in other parts of the country. Suffolk Whites, made at Woolpit, were famous, and even small brickworks such as that at South Elmham St Cross made both red and white bricks, using a distinctive stamp, a cross in the case of South Elmham.

Textiles. Weaving was of course a major industry in both counties in the distant past, and many of our fine churches bear witness to the generosity of the wool merchants. In later times at Haverhill and Syleham drabette, for the making of smocks and other clothing for farm workers, was spun, woven, dyed and made up. The watermill at Syleham was used to power the machines until it was burnt down in 1928. At Glemsford is the only remaining horsehair factory in the country.

Rope Making. A firm of rope makers is still in existence at Haverhill, although the rope-walk is now practically out of use.

Cider. In 1722 Temple Chevallier bequeathed to his cousin, Clement Benjamin Chevallier, a draper and merchant of St Helier, Jersey, property at Aspall in Suffolk. He settled there in 1727, marrying Jane Gurneys, a relative of the Freeman family whose diaries have provided such a wealth of information for this book.

Clement brought over from his former home a stone cider mill, and established orchards of trees from the same source, to ensure the right stock of apples. The old press is now operated only on occasion as a demonstration, but cider is still made, by modern methods. Mention is made elsewhere of the contributions made in various ways by Clement's son, Temple, and his grandson John.

Malting and Brewing. In an area where barley was grown with such success, it was natural that maltings should spring up, but the region supplied not only the local firms but others further afield; Burton-on-Trent was a good customer. During the slack season on the farms, it was common practice for some of the labourers to move to Burton for a spell of work in the maltings there; some even found the area so much to their liking that they eventually settled there.* The old

* For an excellent and detailed study of migrant workers, see Evans, 1970.

established maltings add picturesque interest to the local skyline, and it would be deplorable if this is lost in the interests of too much development. The maltings at Snape have achieved immortality as a concert hall which houses most of the major musical events of the Aldeburgh Festival.

Our breweries tend to lose their identity in the mergers which are in vogue at the present time, but some at least have survived to maintain their own brands of beer.

Fisheries. Two names come to mind in particular as centres of the fishing industries, though of very different types—Lowestoft in Suffolk and Wivenhoe in Essex. Lowestoft has been a fishing port of more than local note since as far back as the fourteenth century.

During the heyday of the herring fisheries, catches were so great that the fisher-girls from Scotland used to come down annually for the season, to gut the herring and pack them in barrels, well salted to preserve them on their long journey to the Baltic and north Europe generally. There was also a trade in bloaters and kippers, and some of the curing sheds are still to be seen.

Wivenhoe was the centre of the oyster fishery, though some of the beds were as far away as Tollesbury, the mature shellfish being brought to storage pits at Wivenhoe, whence they were distributed throughout the eastern counties and London; some even found their way with the herrings to northern Europe.* The annual Oyster Feast is still held in Colchester.

Ship and Boat Building. Fishing boats were built at Lowestoft, as might be expected, and dredgers at Wivenhoe, and the industry gradually increased in importance and spread its range of vessels. Other centres, notably Ipswich in Suffolk and Maldon in Essex, also developed this trade.

* Brown, 1969.

3 Preparing the Land

DRAINAGE (Pls 58–60, 68–9)

The heavy clay soil which covers so much of our region demands thorough drainage for successful cultivation, and the methods used have varied through the ages.

> '*The sede being sowne, waterforow the ground:*
> *that rain when it cummeth, may runne away round.*'

So says Thomas Tusser in *A hundreth good poyntes of husbandry*, writing in 1557 from experience of the poor land of the Cattawade area where Essex and Suffolk meet.

Following generations have preferred to drain before sowing. The Wimbish district of Essex is notable for great advances in drainage technique leading eventually, as will appear, to developments in ploughing too. In view of this, and of the fact that some of the implements used seem to be peculiar to East Anglia, or at least to have originated there, it would seem profitable to give the history of the process in some detail.

Until the introduction of hollow-draining, the land was surface drained, both in Essex and in Suffolk, by the 'Essex ridge and furrow system'. A ridge of thirty-six inches was formed by ploughing two bouts or turns, the share turning up nine inches each round. This was increased in Suffolk to form the stetch of 7 ft 6 ins or 9 ft. As early as 1740, or perhaps earlier, this was supplemented by hollow-draining.* Raynbird,† making a comparison between Suffolk practices in 1803 and 1846, has this to say:

'1803. On wet lands the 3-foot Essex ridge of two bouts is most common, but farmers are beginning to adopt their stetches to their drilling machines.

* Thirsk and Imray, 1958.
† W. and H. Raynbird, 1849.

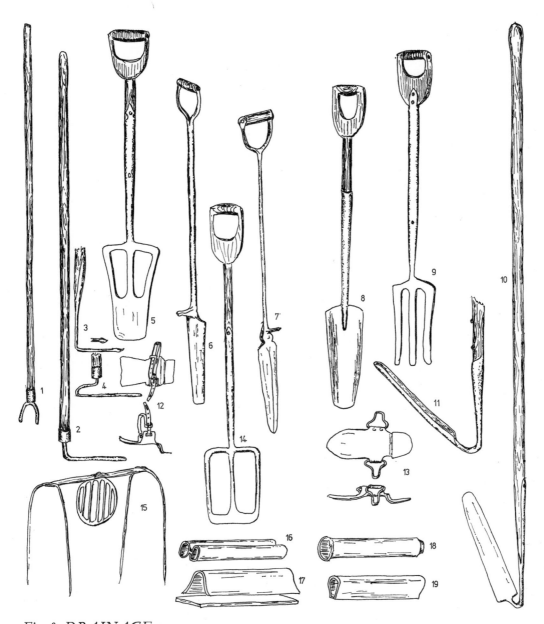

Fig. 8. DRAINAGE

1. Crotch (for ramming filling of bush-drains). 2, 3, 4. Pipe-layers. 5. Top-spade. 6. Bottom-spade (tile-draining). 7. Bottom-spade (bush-draining). 8. Ditching-spade, 'gouge'. 9. Clay-fork. 10. Scoop (tile-draining). 11. Scoop (bush-draining). 12, 13. Drainage-shoes (top and side views). 14. Brick maker's spade (also used for cutting drains). 15. Grid. 16. Drainpipe (double). 17. 'Inverted-U' pipe, and sole. 18. Cylindrical pipe (chamfered to fit one into another). 19. 'Donkey-shoe' pipe. (All $\frac{1}{12}$.)

1846. Nearly all stetches; only a small district near Clare and Haverhill adhere to the ridge system.'

In the last years of the eighteenth century James Young of Clare, Suffolk, described his method of hollow-draining.* He first ploughed two furrows with a 'common plough', leaving a balk between them; he then split the balk with a 'double-breasted' plough† to a depth of 15 or even 20 inches, after which a ditching-spade was used to dig to a depth of a further 15 inches.

The general practice was to dig the first spit with the top-spade, following this with the bottom-spade, which had a narrow or wide cutting edge according to whether bush- or tile-draining was intended; a drainage-shoe was worn to protect the sole of the boot. The scoop, with pointed or wide blade as required, was used for levelling the bottom. Implements other than the traditional spades were also used: the gouge, the brick maker's spade, or the clay-fork.

For bush-draining, brushwood, stubble, straw, vegetable haulms and even stones were used as filling; Thomas Potts records the use of straw-rope. The filling was pressed down with a crotch.

Tile-draining is recorded as early as 1817.‡ An early type was the inverted-U, usually laid on a flat sole. The donkey-shoe tile seems to be a version of this, with sides compressed and base attached; it could be fitted into the narrow bush-draining trench.§ Various machines for the cutting of drains were invented, but proved unsatisfactory. On a farm at Exning, near Newmarket, a grid secured by a four-legged spiked frame was placed in the path of the drain to prevent the passage of small mammals.

The great invention of the time, however, was the mole-plough, devised by Adam Scott and improved by various designers, especially one Lumbert. It was operated by a team of eight women, four at a time, working two windlasses; in one day they could cut 'three hundred perches of drain eighteen inches deep, each perch containing five yards and a half'.

It was a short step from this machine to the horse-gin, an excellent example of which, from Wimbish, may be seen at the Abbot's Hall Museum. This could be anchored in the middle of a field, and the drains cut radially. The next stage was the employment of a traction engine, and it was from this that the idea of ploughing by steam arose, being first attempted about 1820.

* Potts, 1808; and Young, 1797 and 1813.
† Probably this was the origin of the ridging plough.
‡ Trist, 1971.
§ W. and H. Raynbird, 1849.

With all this fertility of inventiveness, it is surprising to find the earlier methods of draining, and also ploughing, persisting to such a marked extent well over a hundred years later.

PLOUGHING AND HARROWING (Pls 70–9)

It was the necessity for draining thoroughly which dictated the form in which ploughing was carried out, dividing each field into 'lands' (*stetches* in Suffolk), slightly elevated in the centre, and divided by open furrows by which surface water could escape. These furrows were also designed to provide passage for the wheels of the drills and other implements, and for the horses which drew them. It was therefore of considerable importance that they should be drawn with the greatest degree of accuracy. It was the task of the first horseman to draw the first furrow of the stetch, turning so that the second furrow would meet the first to form a ridge. Frequently he would be followed by the least experienced member of the team, any deviation in whose work would then be corrected by being followed by a more experienced man. When the stetches were completed, the open furrows were 'tommed up' with a ridging plough with a double mould-board so as to keep them well defined.

The number of stetches depended on the nature of the land; light land called for fewer and wider stetches than heavy clay, which needed more effective drainage. As the ploughs usually employed cut a 9-inch furrow, a stetch might consist of twelve furrows—a 9-foot stetch, usual in Suffolk—or more or less according to need.

The accuracy of the work was a matter of great pride; it would be subject to the critical inspection of fellow workers. To quote Arthur Young (1813):

'The ploughmen are remarkable for straight furrows; and also for drawing them by the eye to any object, usually a stick whitened by peeling, either for water cuts, or for laying out broad ridges, called here *stitches*; and a favourite amusement is ploughing such furrows, as candidates for a hat, or pair of breeches, given by alehouse-keepers, or subscribed among themselves, as a prize for the straightest furrow. The skill of many of them in this work is remarkable.'

Even though the use of the horse-plough has now disappeared except in rare cases, these drawing matches are still popular.

The drawing of a straight furrow was not, however, merely a matter of pride; it was an essential element in the whole process of successful cultivation. The drills

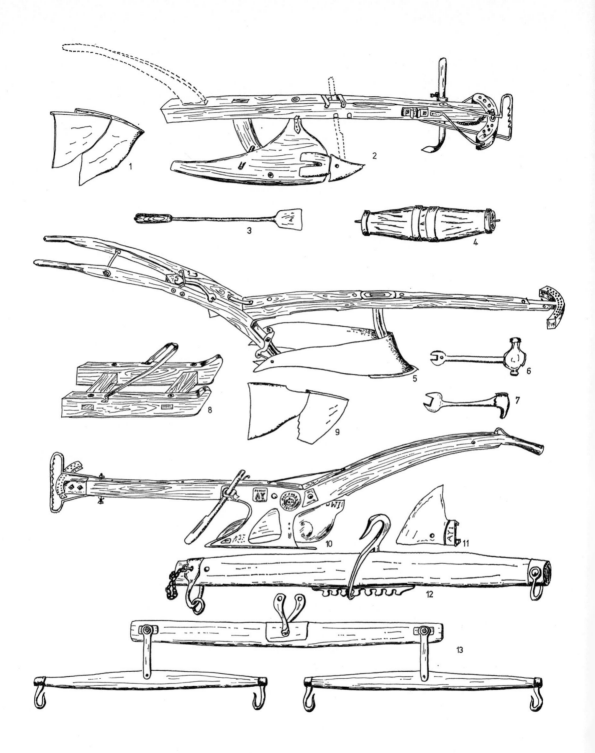

and other implements used were made specifically to run in the furrows, and to be kept off the ploughed land. It needed but a few inches of error to create difficulties for the drill.

The term stetch would seem, originally at least, to be exclusive to Suffolk, for in the diaries of Charles Freeman, written between 1820 and 1830, the word does not occur during his time at Thorpe Abbots, in Norfolk, but comes into regular use after he had moved to Stowupland Hall in Suffolk.

William and Hugh Raynbird, writing in 1849, attributed the success of arable farming in Suffolk in large measure to the system of ploughing employed, and to the development of the manufacture in the county of ploughs and other agriculture implements.

'. . . The universal system of ploughing with *two horses*, however stiff the soil may be; and as the Suffolk poet says,

> "*No wheels support the diving pointed share,*
> *No groaning ox is doomed to labour there,*
> *No* helpmates *teach the docile steed his road,*
> *Alike unknown the* ploughboy *and his goad,*
> *But, unassisted through each toilsome day,*
> *With smiling brow the ploughman cleaves his way.*"
> Bloomfield's *Farmer's Boy*, 1798.'

Bloomfield's picture does not appear to be entirely accurate; there is evidence that in Essex at least it was the practice at one time for the horseman to lead the team,* the ploughman guiding the plough, but in Suffolk the term horseman is synonymous with ploughman. The swing plough, wheelless, enjoyed great popularity in both counties, and although oxen were used in ploughing, their employment was more usual with the harrow.

* However, this practice would seem to have been limited to a short period in the latter part of the nineteenth century, for Arthur Young (1807) writes: 'The general plough-team is two horses, driven by the ploughman by means of a cord.'

Fig. 9. PLOUGHING
1. Share from swing plough by Bentall of Maldon. 2. Early swing plough with wooden mouldboard. 3. Plough-staff, plough-spud. 4. 'Pup-roll' (to span the gap between twin rolls). 5. Ridging plough, 'tom-plough', by Warren of Goldhanger. 6, 7. Plough-spanners, with hammer-heads. 8. 'Slod' or 'sled' (to convey plough from place to place). 9. Share from Cornish and Lloyds' GCB plough. 10. Ransomes AY swing plough (1835). 11. Share from Ransomes AY plough. 12. 'Snotch' pummeltree. 13. Pummeltree and whippletrees.
(Nos. 2, 4, 5, 8 and 10, $\frac{1}{24}$; remainder $\frac{1}{12}$.)

Arthur Young wrote that 'the ploughs of Essex . . . are swing and wheeled, the latter generally on dry land and the former on wet, but in some districts swing ploughs are used on all soils'. The relative merits were a theme for discussion by the various Farmers' Clubs, but the swing plough enjoyed great popularity. Ransomes AY (1835) was a swing plough, though occasionally equipped with a wheel. A peg let into the stilt near the handle facilitated turning at the end of the furrow, but if this did not give enough purchase the ploughman would cut a stout branch and insert this into the angle between stilt and mouldboard; Cornish and Lloyds' GCB plough had a bracket for a detachable second stilt.

It is notable that the popularity of the AY plough was such that although Ransomes introduced their iron YL wheeled plough in 1843, so great was the demand for the AY that round about 1860 the firm of Bendall, of Woodbridge, manufactured a plough which they called the AY; it was designed to take Ransomes' spares. One of these ploughs, dated 1869, was used by George Turner at Dial Farm, Earl Soham, in 1905.

Ransomes' ploughs were used throughout Suffolk, Norfolk and Essex, but the last county had its own very successful Goldhanger swing plough, made by Warren the blacksmith in the village of Goldhanger, and later by Bentall at Maldon. Both Bentalls and Warren also produced double-handed ridging ploughs with fixed mouldboards, the so-called tom-ploughs or double-toms, used not only for tomming up the stetches, but for opening up trenches for potatoes, and later for earthing up.

Robert Ransome is famous for his invention of the process of *chilling* cast iron; he produced the first chilled cast-iron share in 1803, the advantage of which over the wrought-iron share was that it was to all intents and purposes self-sharpening.

Another invention by a Suffolk man was the slade, or sole, which helped to keep the plough on an even keel.

The YL plough, as other iron ploughs, was so constructed as to allow the larger wheel to run in the furrow, with a smaller land-wheel running on the surface. One of the disadvantages of these heavy ploughs was the tendency, on heavy land, of the land-wheel to sink in and so impede the passage of the plough. This was obviated by the substitution of a *foot*, an iron bar flattened at the distal end and turned at right angles, so that it slid over the surface. A foot is also found on a very early wooden swing plough, with wooden mouldboard and iron share but no slade, now in the Abbot's Hall Museum.

At a recent drawing-match, a Ransomes' RNE match plough, a development of the Newcastle plough, was fitted with both wheel and foot, either of which could be raised or lowered for use as desired.

43. Horse stocks used to secure a restive animal, at the forge, Belstead.

44. Shoeing a horse in the 'traviss' of a forge at Bramfield.

45. Arthur ('Trixie') Drewry and Albert ('Smoker') Palmer quartering flints into workable pieces. Both men were employed on this work by Herbert Edwards, landlord of the Flintknapper's Arms.

46. Using the leggatt to drive in the thatch; on the left can be seen untrimmed reed, thatch-pins, etc.

47. Straw is used for the coping, and the sways or liggers are placed in a criss-cross pattern.

48. The final effect seen on the dormer windows: reed thatch, straw coping and eaves neatly trimmed.

49. *Bundling osiers with the horse.*

50. *T. T. Mullins, osier basketmaker, using the lap-board.*

51. *Plaiting rushes; the Debenham Rush Weavers at work.*

BRIAN PALFREY MAKING A CASK.

52. 'Raising' the cask; beating down the hoops with the driver.

53. Topping the cask with the adze.

54. Shaping the head with the heading-knife.

55. Smoothing the head with the heading-swift.

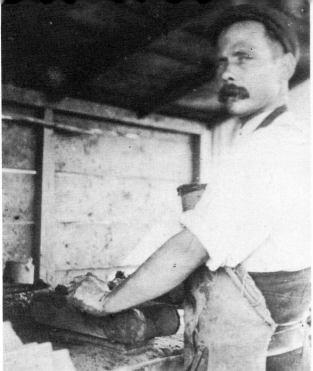

BRICK MAKING AT TUDDENHAM.

56. Moulding a brick, 1901; the works closed down in 1903.

57. Stacking bricks in the kiln, August 1900.

58. Loading bricks ready for 'ripening', 1901.

DRAINING AT CULPHO, 1911.

59. Using the gouge.

60. Levelling with the scoop.

61. Laying the pipes.

62. *The horse-operated cider press brought from Jersey by Clement Chevallier in 1727. (Courtesy East Anglian Daily Times.)*

63. *Watercolour drawing by H. G. Cobbold, millwright, depicting the dressing of a millstone, using millbill and thrift; Bradfield St George smock mill.*

64. *The upper stone of a pair at the Debenham tower mill lifted off by crane in readiness for dressing.*

65. *The smock mill at Wortham.*

66. *Post mill at Drinkstone, Suffolk, built in 1689; round-house added about a hundred years later.*

67. *Rushbroke's watermill on the River Gipping at Bramford, 1955.*

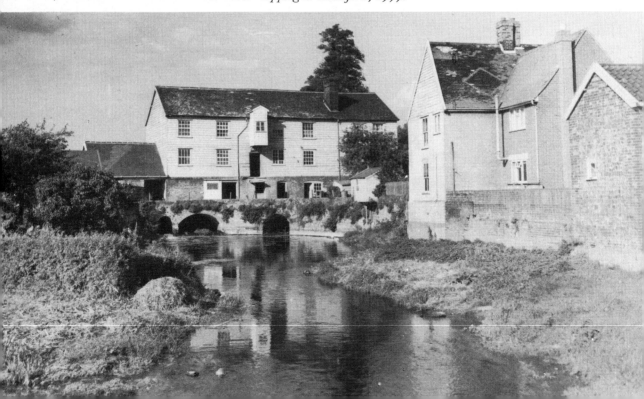

The YLD series of Ransomes ploughs, for double-furrow work, were necessarily increased in weight by the extra mouldboard; turning at the end of the furrow was made more difficult in consequence. This was overcome by substituting for the land-wheel a bowl-wheel ('pudden' wheel in Suffolk, from its resemblance to a pudding-basin). The ploughman bore down on the left-hand stilt, thus causing the weight to be taken on the bowl, on which the plough could be swung with comparative ease; an angled bracket projecting from the stilt prevented it from falling on to its side.

Two horses were generally used, harnessed side by side, a pummeltree attached to the hake of the plough providing attachment for two whippletrees to which traces were linked. The hake allowed adjustment up or down according to the size of the horses, the T-piece controlling the degree of lateral pull. A snotch pummel-tree fitted with a ratchet provided a means of regulating the difference in pulling power of the two horses. Three horses, or a combination of horses and oxen, could be used by fitting a compensating gear.

The manufacture of ploughs and other implements was not confined to the larger firms. Daniel Cameron of Bungay produced the 'East Anglian Plough' in the latter part of the nineteenth century. A representation of the plough appears on his bill-head and that of his successor, H. N. Rumsby. It appears to differ in no essential detail from Ransomes YL. In the account book of W. Rogers, of Boundary Farm, Ilketshall St Margaret, there appears the following entry:

> 'May 5th. 1905. Bought E. H. Plough of
> Mr. H. Rumsby   £4. 15. 0 (complete)   Paid
> 17. 9
> Credit till after Harvest.'

The extra 2s. 9d. would seem to be interest on account of the delayed payment.

Suffolk ploughs were well thought of in Essex, but the traffic was not all one way. William Freeman of Stowupland Hall received on approval, on 29th August 1853, a plough from Bentalls of Maldon, and P. J. O. Trist (1971) tells how G. T. Church of Little Wenham Hall in Suffolk ploughed the greater part of his 600 acres on the 7 ft 6 in. stetch as recently as the beginning of the Second World War, and tommed up the furrows with the wooden-framed Goldhanger plough with double mouldboard.

Fallow land in Suffolk was known as summerland, summerlin, or summertilth, the name being derived from the practice of ploughing and 'over-warting' (cross-ploughing) at least three times during the summer that it was not cropped.* It was then sown with turnips, mangolds or some other root crop.

Charles Freeman recorded in his diary for 5th August 1823: 'B. ploughing Stonham Somertill 3rd. time', and on 26th November he had three men 'ploughing Somertill', and on the 29th 'stetching up at Somertills'. William, his son, gives an even clearer picture:

'1854. Mar. 15. Overwarting Fesdens.
            25. Scarifying and harrowing Fesdens.
            27. Harrowing and scarifying Fesdens.
     Apr.   5. Ctnd. harrowing Fesdens.
            11. . . . men very busy raking and burning Fesdens.
            20. Horsemen ploughing Fesdens 2nd. time overwart.
            25. Scarifying Fesdens.
     June 22. . . . stetching up Fesdens for turnips.
            19. Dent redrilling white turnip seed in Fesdens where misplanted.'

Until the advent of mechanization, the use of heavy ploughs and the end of stetching, the fallow was a regular part of the crop rotation, and might even be a condition of tenancy (Trist 1971).

The use of pummeltree and whippletrees for harnessing a pair of horses has already been described. When three horses were used a supplementary compensating gear of hinged iron bars was added, in order to distribute the load. A heavy spanner, often with a hammer-head, was carried in a slot on one of the stilts of the plough, and a false link was carried by the horseman in case of breakages; these links were made by the blacksmith as required.

For transport from field to field, the plough was mounted on a slod, or sled, a stoutly built wooden sledge with iron runners; occasionally an iron slod with wheels was used.

The harrows used in Suffolk and Essex did not differ materially from those in general use; until well into the present century, they were frequently drawn by oxen. The *Farmers' Magazine* for 1841 reports a discussion which took place at a meeting of the Wrentham Farmers' Club on 'the advantage to be derived from the use of oxen for the purpose of labour, in lieu of horses'. One speaker argued strongly that oxen, after a working life of three years, increased in value, whereas the horse steadily depreciated in value. As is often the case, the meeting gave cautious approval 'that working oxen *may* be used with advantage'.

* Cross-ploughing eight or nine times was usual in Essex, and some farmers ploughed as many as twelve times (Arthur Young).

Harrowing was not completely effective on the heavy soils of our region, and the scarifier, first introduced (as were so many innovations) in Scotland, was successfully modified in Suffolk by Arthur Biddell. The exact form of his first model is not known, but J. Allen Ransome, writing in 1843, describes it as having 'a framing of wood, with tines of wrought iron'. A large wooden implement of harrow type at the Abbot's Hall Museum is of heavy timber, triangular in form, with sides of 8 feet and base of 7 feet; the tines are stout, and project 10 inches; it seems likely that this is an example of the early Biddell scarifier.

Arthur Biddell married Jane Ransome, daughter of Robert, who had already made agricultural history with his chilled-iron plough. Biddell's later scarifiers, made first in wrought iron and later in cast iron, were highly esteemed, and it was in all probability the former that created such interest at the Royal Society's Show (its first) in 1839 at Oxford. It in no way resembled the wooden-framed implement, which had no wheels; both iron versions ran on large rear wheels with two smaller wheels, close together, in front. The wrought-iron model was made in two sizes, with nine or seven blades; the cast-iron scarifier had nine blades, which were interchangeable with hoes. J. Hudson, writing in the *Farmers' Magazine* in July 1847, says: 'During the last spring and summer I have used Biddle's [sic] *improved* scarifiers to great advantage, and certainly save a ploughing by using them for barley, as well as for turnips.'

Another of Biddell's inventions was the Extirpating Harrow, of which Raynbird says that 'it is intended for breaking up land when it is too hard for the heaviest harrows, and for bringing winter fallows into a state of fine tillage. In working summerlands it is calculated, by the shape of its teeth, to bring to the surface all grass and rubbish'.

The name extirpator is given to two widely differing types of implement. Arthur Young illustrates a machine invented by a Mr Hayward, of Stoke Ash, 'for destroying weeds, and clearing ploughed lands for seed'. It has thirteen horizontal triangular blades, rather like those of a horse-hoe, and is drawn behind a wheeled fore-carriage.

Another, later, extirpator, the invention of Robert Fuller of Rushmere, brought out at about the same time as Biddell's scarifier, much more resembles that machine. It has sharp, strongly curved tines, calculated to tackle deep-rooted weeds.

The ordinary light crab- or seed-harrow has varied little over the years; two, three or more sections can be linked by chains, and attached to a draw-bar to which the traces of the horses are hooked.

Until the advent of the tractor, all these implements were drawn by horses or oxen, the latter being shod with two separate plates on each hoof, to allow free action of the 'cloven hoof'. The Suffolk Horse or Suffolk Punch was extensively used in Essex and Norfolk as well as Suffolk, but it was not the only farm horse, especially in Essex where Shires, Clydesdales and Percherons, and crosses between them, still appear in ploughing matches. The Rev. Philip Wright, a recognized authority on the heavy horse, recently told the writer that it was common practice for shires used in the drays of the London brewery companies to find their way eventually to the more relaxed atmosphere of the Essex countryside, where the horse-plough is still extensively employed.

FERTILIZING THE LAND

Until the tractor replaced the horse, farmyard manure, and particularly horse-dung with the admixture of straw used as bedding, formed a very considerable percentage of the fertilizing agents used on the farm.

Other methods were in use, however, from quite early times. Kirby's *Suffolk Traveller* (2nd Edition, 1744) refers to the use of 'Chalk, Clay and Crag', and much later came the dramatic discovery of the value of coprolites. So the farmer, or at least the agriculturist, came to realize the possibilities of making the land help itself.

Reference has already been made to the existence of certain shelly deposits laid down in the shallow seas of the Pliocene and Pleistocene periods, known collectively as 'Crag'. Kirby says of it that it 'is found by Experience to be preferable to the other two and may be had cheaper'. He gives a graphic description of its discovery as a means of improving the land:

'In a Farmer's Yard in *Levington*, close on the Left as you enter from Levington into the Chapel-Field of *Stratton*-Hall, was dug the firft *Crag* or *Shell*, that has been found fo ufeful for improving of Land in this and other Hundreds in the Neighbourhood. For though it appears from Books of Agriculture, that the like Manure has been long fince ufed in the *West* of *England*, it was not ufed here till this Discovery was cafually made by one *Edmund Edwards*, about the Year 1718. This Man being covering a Field with Muck out of his Yard, and wanting a Load or two to finifh it, carried fome of the Soil that laid near his Muck, tho' it look'd to him to be no better than *Sand*; but obferving the Crop to be beft where he laid that, he was from thence encouraged to carry more of it the next Year; and the Succefs he had, encouraged others to do the like.

'This ufeful *Soil* has been found in great Plenty upon the Sides of fuch Vales as may reaſonably be ſuppoſed to have been waſhed by the Sea; towards which ſuch light Shells might be naturally carried, either at *Noah's* Flood, or by the Force of the Tides to ſome Places ſince forſaken by the Sea.'

Arthur Young, in his *Farmer's Tour Through the East of England* (1771), tells how he tested it:

'I brought away half a bushel, and have since tried it in strong vinegar, but it has not the least effervescence nor any ebullition; and yet it undoubtedly enriches the soil far more than any marl, for the farmers here lay on but 10 or 12 cart-loads an acre, and the effect is amazingly great; with this uncommon circumstance the soil is ever after greatly the better for it; nor do they in 12 or 15 years, as is common with such small quantities of marl, find the benefit declining fast. But there is a strong notion among them that the land can only be cragged once; if it is after-wards repeated, no advantage is found from it. This part of my intelligence I doubt very much, and especially as they find it very advantageous to form com-posts of crag and dung, which they practise much, carting the dung to the crag pits, and there making the compost-tips, turning it over twice, and sometimes thrice. The redder the crag is the better they reckon it. The effect of it is so great that, on breaking up the poor heaths of this county, they have had a succession of exceed-ingly fine crops of all sorts from such parts as they have manured with it, while at the same time other parts unmanured have scarcely yielded the seed again. The farmers here are very attentive to all sorts of manures; they raise large quantities of farm-yard manure, and cart it all on to crops and mix it either with crag or virgin mould, and this universally.'

Crag was also much used to bring marshlands into arable production, and the marsh soil was itself carried to the sandy uplands.

Chalk was transported long distances to the light lands of the east of the region, but a more characteristic process was that known as claying. The Boulder Clay which covers such a large area of the region contains a considerable admixture of chalk, and when broken up and mixed with farmyard manure, gave a well balanced and valuable fertilizer.

Raynbird gives a detailed account of the method employed in digging and pre-paring the clay. A pit was dug until the clay was exposed, usually about a foot or so below the surface. Digging was regulated so as to form a gradual slope for the horses and carts used for transport.

'As soon as a sufficient depth is obtained the plan of operations is altered; for instead of picking and digging they now proceed to make what are termed "falls", in a manner which is well known to all excavators: this is done by picking or undermining at the bottom for a sufficient distance along the side, and at the extremities of the undermined part, a perpendicular crevice is picked out from the top to the bottom. This having been completed, clay wedges shod with iron are driven at top with a heavy mallet or beetle, and this being continued for a short time the clay splits down perpendicularly. In this manner as much soil is "raised" as will be filled into carts by three men in a day's work. Men employed in filling usually "raise" (if falling down may be called raising) the clay when the horses are resting, as after they have left off for the day.'

Filling and spreading the clay were paid the rate of $2\frac{1}{2}d.$ to $3d.$ per load. The work was sometimes done on contract, by measuring the pit after completion. Spreading was paid at the rate of $7d.$ per yard if carted 1 furlong, with $1d.$ for each additional furlong. Ten yards a day per man was considered a good day's work.

After spreading, frost helped to break the clods, and the process was accelerated either by manual labour or by the use of Crosskill's clod-roller.

Clay was applied to the land at 30 to 40 cubic yards to the acre, or more on heathland. It was also used on fenland, as it 'consolidates the loose peaty soil'.

As the ploughing up of former pasture increased with the development of arable farming, it was found beneficial, and in fact deemed essential, to cover the broken up pasture with clay; this accounts for the large number of clay pits throughout every heavy-land parish.

On 11th November 1854 William Freeman of Stowupland Hall wrote in his diary: 'Drilling Clog wheat on further Damants and sowing on Packard's manure Broadcast.' This is the first recorded instance known to the present writer of the use of a fertilizer developed by a process which was to lead to the establishment of one of the major industries associated with agriculture.

John Stevens Henslow was born in 1796, and graduated from St John's College, Cambridge, in mathematics in 1818. In 1822 he was appointed to the Chair of Mineralogy in the University; he took Holy Orders in 1824, and became Professor of Botany in 1827. It was Henslow who obtained for Charles Darwin the post of naturalist in H.M.S. *Beagle* in 1831. In 1837 he became Rector of Hitcham in Suffolk,* and took up residence there in 1839, remaining until his death in 1861.

In the course of his studies Henslow discovered that coprolites, the fossil dung of prehistoric animals, were rich in phosphates. There were extensive beds of these fossils in Suffolk, and Henslow suggested that Edward Packard of Snape should examine their possibilities as a source of the mineral. This he did with great success,

* Not Hitchin, Herts., as stated by Trist (1971).

first using a converted flour mill, then moving to Ipswich in 1849, and establishing a factory at Bramford in 1857. Other firms were interested in the project and ultimately amalgamation between Packards, Fisons and the firm of Prentice of Stowmarket laid the foundation for the present Fisons group.

After the establishment of Fisons' factory at Cliff Quay, Ipswich, the ready availability of imported pyrites as a source of superphosphates rendered the processing of coprolites unprofitable and the intriguing situation in which ancient animals had fertilized the fields on the modern farm ceased to exist.

4 Sowing and Growing

(Pls 80–5)

Whether it is owing to the fact that early methods have persisted over a long period, or because the implements themselves are of such durable materials, we do not have to rely on second-hand accounts for a description of most of them, although we shall delve into past records to learn more of them in use; there are still those who can demonstrate this.

Even broadcast sowing using the seed tray or seed box was a skilfully controlled operation, performed not by an outward fling from the centre but by sweeping the arm outward and backward, and releasing the grain as it came round forward. Timed so that foot and hand worked in harmony, it resulted in a regular spread, and little wastage or overlap. The tray is made from a strip of willow, a resilient wood, bent round to form a 'kidney' shape fitting the curve of the body; the base is of hessian or linen, and it is supported by straps or rope running from the sides round the neck of the sower.

'Seedlip' is a term applied to this and also to the 'seed fiddle', especially to the earlier form, similarly fashioned to fit the curve of the body. This instrument was equipped with a container for the seed, which flowed on to a circular plate with radial flanges, which flung off the seed as it was rotated clockwise and anticlockwise by the action of a thong round the spindle, activated by a 'bow'. An early type in the Abbot's Hall collection has a window through which the state of the seed can be seen; unlike most of the later models, it is worked by the left hand.

The *dibbler*, *dibble* or *debble* (in the Freeman diaries) was a stout iron rod, expanding at the distal end into a torpedo-shaped head, the diameter varying, thicker for beans than for corn. Raynbird's description of its use is so excellent in every way that it is worth quoting in full:

'Dibbling is done by men who use two iron dibblers, one in each hand, walking backwards; one man finds employment for three children dropping the seed; the cost from 5*s*. to 8*s*. per acre; the distance between the holes varies from 3 to 5 inches, that between the rows from 4½ to 9; thus one row of holes is put in the centre of each furrow, or two runs on a furrow; some put 16 runs on a 12-furrow stetch, putting two rows on the wide furrows, and only one on the narrow ones at the ridge end furrow. After seed is deposited the land is harrowed.

Among the advantages of dibbling are:

    1st. The employment of the labourer and his family.

    2nd. The sowing of seed (from 6 to 7 packs usually dibbled).

    3rd. That the straw grows stiffer, and is not liable to be lodged.'

In his comparison of methods used at various periods, Raynbird finds that in 1803 it was stated that 'peas should always be dibbled', whilst by 1846 'peas should always be drilled'.

In October 1823 Charles Freeman is 'setting wheat in Horse Close . . . 3 pr. debbles', and later '5 pr. debbles'. In November 1825 he 'debbled acorns in on the top of Bank round Yards. Two in a foot'; in March, 1827, 'debbling beans in Stonham field after Ploughs'.

The first mention of the use of a drill in these diaries occurs in the following April, when he is drilling barley, and again in March 1828, 'Began drilling Barley in Calf's Pightles'. In November 1829 he has 'M. Bland drilling wheat' and in addition '3 pr. Debbles at work in Calf's Pightles', and on the following day '*drilling* and *setting*'. Throughout he appears to use the term *setting* when the dibbles are used, as opposed to *drilling*.

William Freeman, son of Charles, in 1853 is still using the dibble for beans, but his use of the drill for all other purposes is increasing.

Writing in 1803, Arthur Young speaks highly of dibbling, and recommends the following procedure for beans: '. . . a two-horse roll should follow the ploughs, to level the land for the dibblers, which should be harrowed twice after the beans are deposited; when the beans are all up, they are rolled, and in ten days or more, harrowed with heavy harrows'. He also comments that treading by the children who drop in the seed, so far from being harmful, is one of the factors 'to which many attribute the superiority of dibbling'.

A rhyme, oft-quoted, tells of this process:

> '*Four seeds in a hole*
> *One for the rook, one for the crow,*
> *One to rot, and one to grow.*'

In another version, the second line reads:

> '*One for the Parson, one for the crow*'

a reference to the practice of levying tithes.

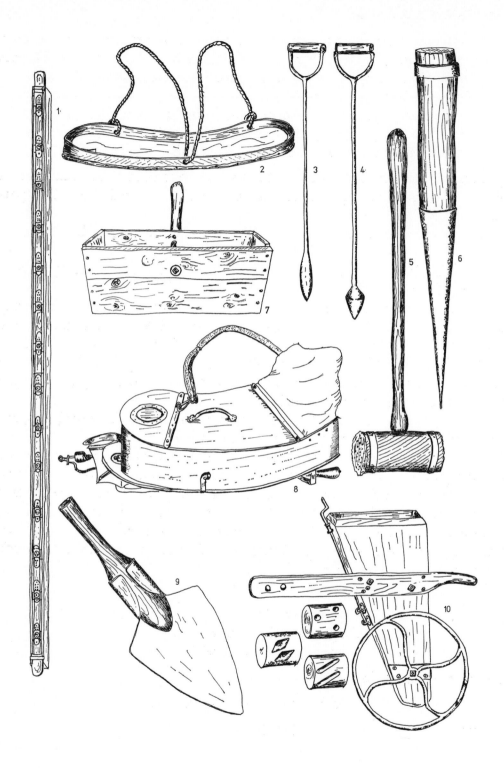

Arthur Young collected the views of a number of local farmers on the value of dibbling as compared with drilling. It is recommended by some for 'wheat, beans and pease' . . . 'and latterly barley and oats, which are thought to answer well; the expence 10*s*. 6*d*. an acre without any allowances'; or again, 'Dibbling wheat maintains its reputation and increases it—price 9*s*. per acre, and beer'. It did depend, however, on the state of the ground, and on the time of year at which the various crops were planted. One writer says: 'Barley is seldom dibbled, by reason the land is so dry in April, that the holes will run in, and not stand open to receive the seed.'

By 1803 Arthur Young found that drilling was very well established in Suffolk, even on the heavy, wet land, whereas in Norfolk it was confined almost exclusively to the sandy soils. It was no doubt this state of affairs which led to the great development of drill manufacture in Suffolk. P. J. O. Trist (1971) quotes the experience of a writer in the *New East Anglia*, in 1901, who had the task of repairing 'old Norfolk block drills . . . about the most unserviceable instrument of its kind which could be conceived'. It dated from 1788, and like so many gadgets in agriculture, was designed by a parson, the Rev. Cooke of Semer. Trist goes on to relate how one Robert Wardley of Peasenhall, a farmer, aroused the interest of James Smyth, who had set up as a wheelwright in Peasenhall. Smyth, after some failures, eventually produced a drill in which the coulters were provided with separate levers, and not, as in the block drill, fixed to a single transverse beam. By about 1830, Smyth had turned out a very successful steerage drill; one of these, now in the collection at the Abbot's Hall Museum, was used by the Saunders family of Cranley Hall, Eye, until 1964, when its use was discontinued only because Mr Saunders ceased to carry out his own drilling, and employed a contractor. The usual practice was to use four horses walking in the furrows, but in this case three were harnessed to the drill, by means of a pummeltree, compensating gear, and three whippletrees. Later a tractor was used, with a draw-bar. About 1860 Smyths introduced the 'Nonpareil' drill, which continued in production almost until the firm closed down in 1965.

The plough-drill, attached to the plough so that ploughing and sowing were

Fig. 10. SOWING, MANURING
1. Manual broadcast seed drill. 2. Seed tray. 3. Dibble, dibbler, 'debble' (for corn). 4. Dibble for beans. 5. 'Beetle' (for driving the wedge when mining clay). 6. Wedge (for use with 5). 7. Seed box (also used for 'sowing' fertilizer). 8. Seed fiddle (an early type with 'window' for viewing seed). 9. Dung spade. 10. Plough-drill (locally called 'bean-barrow'), with barrels for corn (round pits) and beans (elongated pits).
(No. 1, $\frac{1}{18}$; barrels of plough-drill, $\frac{1}{6}$; remainder, $\frac{1}{12}$.)

combined in one operation, was known locally as the bean-drill or bean-barrow, although the original labels still adhering to examples in the Museum collection describe them as corn-drills. The apex of the triangular body is fitted with brushes and a cylindrical barrel with pits, round for corn and obliquely elongate for beans, made of wood or iron, and interchangeable. Beans were also sown by hand in drills drawn with the bean-rake, which had four tines rather like miniature scythe-blades, set about 3 inches apart.

Raynbird illustrates a type of wheeled dibble, a wheel of 18 inches diameter with dibble points 7 inches apart to make the holes; the seed was dropped with a sharp jerk from a bottle with a large quill inserted through the cork. If the implement proved too light, a weight was hung from the cross-bar of the shafts.

The broadcast seed barrow consists of a long narrow box with hinged lid, supported transversely across a wheeled frame. It was drawn by one man and steered by another by means of shafts. One seen in operation at Gislingham a few years ago was so propelled, although on the following day the haulier had apparently decided that the going was too rough, and was using a tractor. The box may be 12 feet in length or even longer. Two versions are found: that in common use has brushes which expel the seed through a series of perforated plates; the other has a barrel as in the horse-drill, with wheels with cups, probably intended for corn rather than seed.

Quite the most unusual broadcast drill, and one which seems to be exclusive to Suffolk, consists of a long narrow box, with sliding lids meeting midway, rather like a child's pencil-box. These are opened out and the box filled with seed. In the lids, if one can call them that, is a series of copper slides, perforated so that they can be adjusted to allow one, two, three or four seeds to escape. The box is then inverted and carried in front of the body, and shaken from side to side as the sower walks forward. This drill is found in two lengths, 9 ft and 12 ft, perhaps corresponding to the width of the stetch. An apparently early example has no slides but simply holes, and others open from the top, with slides in the base. Where these have been found lying about in the barn, their owners often do not even know their use.

Drilling, harrowing and oblique harrowing, after sowing, and particularly after dibbling, were followed by rolling with the wooden horse-roll, made in two sections which could be used together or separately; when paired, they were followed by a 'pup-roll', a short stout roller, thicker in the middle than at the ends (called by Raynbird a 'follower') which took care of the interval not covered by the pair.

Two major enemies of the growing crops were the weeds and the birds. To

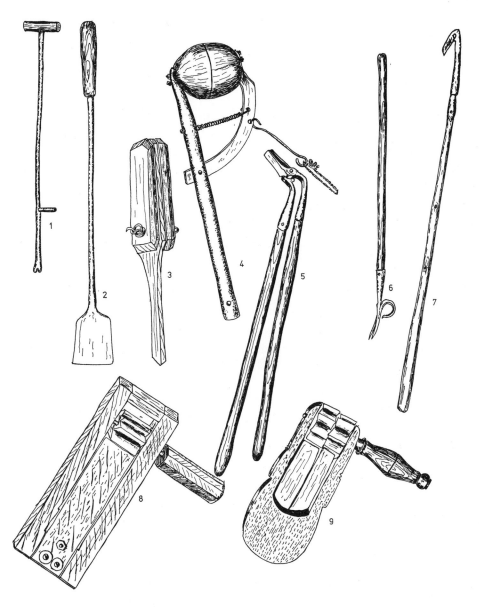

Fig. 11. CROP PROTECTION

1. Weeding-iron. 2. Spud (often a plough-staff was used). 3. Bird-scaring 'clappers'. 4. Bird-scarer (made from a coconut). 5. Weeding-tongs, 'Neps'. 6. Dock-lifter. 7. Thistle-hook (made from the tip of an old scythe-blade). 8, 9. Bird-scarers.
(No. 5, $\frac{1}{12}$; remainder, $\frac{1}{6}$.)

cope with the latter, until methods of pre-treatment of the seed proved effective, a local boy was often employed and equipped with a pair of 'clappers', or the rattle now more familiar as the weapon of football fans, to scare away the birds.

Hand-hoeing and horse-hoeing have both been practised since the early years of the nineteenth century, and the implement varies to suit the crop; the broad arrow-shaped blades of the horse-hoe, adjustable to the width of the rows in later models, bear no resemblance to the curved prongs of the beet-scoop, designed to weed between the rows without damaging the roots.

Hand-hoes were made with interchangeable blades, and special tools were developed to cope with individual weeds; the dock-lifter, with a spur to allow pressure of the foot to ensure deep penetration; the thistle-hook, often made by the blacksmith from the broken tip of a discarded scythe blade; and perhaps the most remarkable of all, the weeding-tongs or 'neps', of which the *Farmers' Magazine* for 1848 has this to say:

'The thistles and docks are the chief weeds ... and these are eradicated by different instruments. Some use a spade-like [tool] for the purpose but as this only separates the roots, it does not prevent their rapid growth subsequently. By far the best mode is to pull them up by the roots. The instrument used most successfully for this is provincially called "Neps".'

That both this and the thistle-hook were in use as far back as the early sixteenth century is vouched for by Fitzherbert in his *Booke of Husbandrie*:

'Ye chyef instruments for weeding, a paier of tonges made of wood, and in the farther end it is nicked to hold the weed faster ... if it be dry wether then must ye have a wedying hoke with a rocket set upon a lytle staffe a yard longe. And this hoke would be wel steled and grounde sharpe bothe behynde and before, and in his other hande he hath a forked stycke a yarde long'.

So also Thomas Tusser:

'*In May get a weed-hook, a crotch and a glove,
and weed out such weeds, as the corn do not love.*'

The later version of the weeding-tongs has jaws of iron or steel, but even so, only use will bring conviction of the possibility of exerting enough pull with such an unlikely-seeming tool to uproot a stubborn dock or thistle. A spud, also used for weeding, differs little from the plough-staff, and no doubt both found alternative uses.

Nevertheless, no amount of careful preparation of the land, planned sowing, and attention afterwards, would produce good crops without good quality seed. A classic instance of the thought which went into this is the discovery of what came to be called 'Chevallier Barley'. As in the case of Henslow's researches into the value of coprolites as manure, it was once more a parson who was responsible, and moreover one of a family of churchmen interested in agriculture. The Rev. John Chevallier, M.D., came of a family who had owned the village of Aspall since 1702.* His grandfather, Clement Benjamin Chevallier, as already stated, settled in Aspall in 1727, and married Jane, daughter of Nathaniel Gurneys of Kenton. They had six children, only one of whom survived: Temple Chevallier, Fellow of Magdalene College, Cambridge, and rector of Badingham, Cransford and Aspall. Temple was a great friend of Arthur Young, who greatly admired his contributions to agriculture, especially his experiments on turnips and cabbages, and his success with dairy cattle. Dr John was the fifth of his twelve children; he presented himself to the living of Aspall in 1817, and followed his father in his interest in agriculture, although this was not his only interest outside his parish work; at Aspall House he founded a mental home for six patients, for he was a Doctor of Medicine.

His discovery of the new strain of barley which bears his name was described in a MS. document of 1845, transcribed from an account given by Mr Sam Dove and dated 22nd April 1835. It is given in full by Joan Thirsk† and also by Walter Tye, but in the interests of accuracy, it seems appropriate to repeat it here:

'About 10 to 15 years since John Andrewes, a labourer of Mr. Edward Dove of Ulveston Hall, Debenham, had been threshing barley and on his return home at night he complained of his feet being very uneasy. On taking off his shoes he discovered in one of them part of a very fine ear of barley. It struck him as being particularly so, and was careful to have it preserved. He afterwards planted it in his garden and on the following year Dr. and Mr. Charles Chevallier coming to Andrewes cottage to inspect some repairs going on (the cottage belonging to the Doctor) saw three or four ears of the barley growing, he requested it might be kept for him when ripe. The Doctor sowed a small ridge with the produce thus obtained and kept it by itself until he was able to plant an acre and from this acre the produce was 11½ coombs, now about 9 years since. This was again planted and from the increase thence arising he began to dispose of it & from that time it

* A letter in the *East Anglian Daily Times*, 3rd March 1971, from Miss Teresa Chevallier, gives the genealogy.
† Thirsk and Imray, 1958.

has been gradually getting into repute. It is now well known in most of the corn markets in the kingdom and also in many parts of the continent and called after the Doctor's name, the Chevallier Barley.'

Arthur Young records that few varieties of wheat were used in Suffolk, 'the common red, the white, and the bearded, also called *rivets*, and which is sown chiefly on wet cold lands'. In *The British Farmers Cyclopaedia* (1808) this last is called *rivels*, and it is said of both the brown and the white varieties that they ripen late in the season and are 'so coarse and steely as to be unfit for making bread unless mixed with a large proportion of a better sort of flour'. William Freeman was growing red, white and clog wheat in the 1850s; clog wheat is another name for bearded wheat. Although clog wheat fetched a poorer price than the red, he evidently found it worth while to grow some of it on his land, much of which could well be classed as wet and cold.

5 Harvesting

(Pls 86–111)

No operation on the farm has seen such radical changes over the years as the harvesting of crops. Until the introduction of the combine-harvester rather over forty years ago, the harvest field presented a busy scene, with every available worker and the wives of many of them all finding work to do. In these days one solitary man, perched aloft on a 'combine', will spend days without seeing another soul. No longer do the graceful stooks stand in serried ranks to await the harvest wagon. Either the uninspiring spectacle of bales of straw meets the eye, or the straw is left as it is cut until time is found to set it alight, to the discomfort of the passer-by—a menace to the motorist if the field adjoins a highway—or the mortal peril of the life of the hedgerows, both plant and animal.

When food-gathering first gave place to planned cultivation, the harvest was gathered in by means of the flint sickle, the reaper grasping a handful of the growing corn, and literally sawing it off. This practice continued even after the introduction of metal, until a very precise date, 1840, at any rate so far as wheat was concerned, when the scythe came into use for cereal crops in most areas. In Suffolk, however, the horse-mower was adapted, by the addition of a rack to gather the cut corn, for use for crops other than grass, and in some parts directly succeeded the sickle.

There is evidence that some crops, other than wheat, were mown with the scythe earlier than 1840. In the diaries of Charles Freeman of Stowupland, reference is made to *mowing* barley in 1823 and 1824, and both barley and oats in 1829. *Mowing* is a term usually reserved for the use of the scythe, *reaping* when the sickle is used. Charles never talks of mowing wheat, although the word he uses is cutting, not reaping.

Edward Moor (1823) gives *shear* as a term for reaping corn, and an entry in the Freeman diaries in 1821 records the arrival of '12 Shearers after Dinner', and on the following day they are 'Shearing wheat'.

In Suffolk, the change from sickle to scythe did not come without some serious debate, and the *Farmers' Magazine* reports discussions held by the Farmers' Clubs

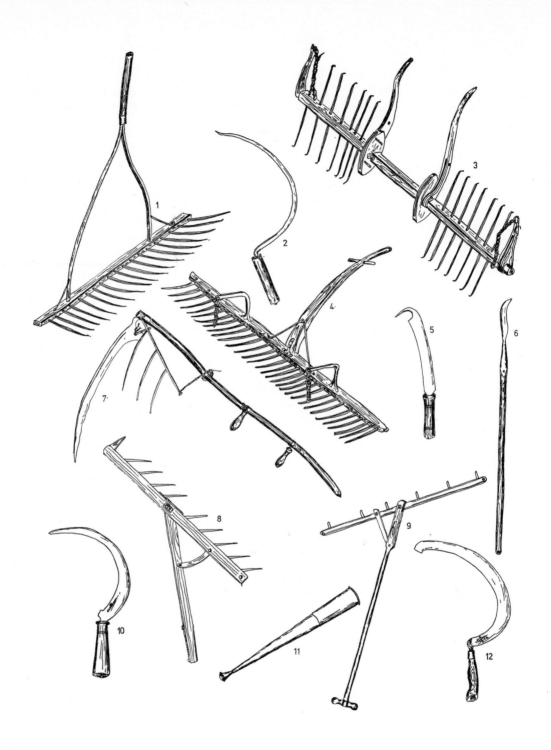

at Hadleigh, Framlingham and Ixworth. In favour of the use of the scythe were the facts that the work was done more quickly, and therefore more cheaply; the sheaves were less tightly tied, and dried more rapidly; the straw was of superior quality, and made better manure. At the Ixworth meeting, however,

'it was argued that mowing was a slovenly way, and had not the neatness of appearance of reaped wheat, and that by getting *all* the corn off the land, you leave nothing for the gleaners; and as gleaning has been allowed from time immemorial, it ought not to be done away with, and indeed it is always looked forward to by the poor people as an assistance in paying off the necessary debts they may have contracted. These objections were met by stating that, as the labourers oftentimes purposely strewed corn while reaping it, mowing was absolutely necessary in self-defence, and that the farmer had every right to all he could grow on his land; that, though gleaning was certainly of very ancient date, yet it never had, either by enactment or otherwise, been rendered lawful, and that the quantity of corn obtained by gleaning off a large farm, was of very serious consequence.'

When the corn was laid by stormy weather a form of sickle with plain, not serrated, blade and blunt tip, the bagging-hook, was used. The corn was not then gathered in the left hand, but literally hacked off as low as possible.

Mention has been made of the adaptation of the grass mower for use with corn by the addition of a side rack; this machine is known in Suffolk as the foot-engine or rack-engine. The rack was raised by pressure of the foot on a pedal, and when sufficient corn had been collected for a sheaf, it was lowered and the corn pushed off with a rake with the head angled at 45 degrees so as to rest horizontally on the rack. A two-seater model, drawn by two horses, was also made, when the rake was operated by the second man. Charlie Brundish, born in 1844, started work on his father's farm, Tan Office, near Mendlesham, in 1857. For his first five years the scythe was used, but he graduated to the foot-engine, a one-seater, one-horse model, when he was eighteen. The ejected sheaf was tied by another worker, using a band of straw formed by pulling out a few strands from the sheaf and twisting them into a rope.

Fig. 12. HARVESTING
1. Hobby rake, moggy rake. 2. Serrated sickle. 3. Hay-toppler (a very early type). 4. Swim-rake (for harvesting peas). 5, 6. Pea-makes. 7. Scythe with cradle, for wheat. 8. Arm of sail-reaper (for comparison with 9). 9. Foot-engine rake. 10. Reap-hook. 11. Harvest horn. 12. Bagging-hook. (Nos. 1, 6, 7, 8 and 9, $\frac{1}{24}$; 3 and 4, $\frac{1}{36}$; remainder, $\frac{1}{12}$.)

It is obvious that the sail-reaper was derived from the foot-engine by attaching a number, four or five, of the angled rakes to a spindle, so that the sheaves were ejected automatically. In Charlie's time the foot-engine was used on the smaller farms, the sail-reaper on those big enough to warrant the cost.

Wheat was invariably made into sheaves and set up in stooks ('shocks' in Suffolk); barley was more often left loose after cutting, although in the early days of the present century it was customary to mow with the scythe the barley to be used for malting, and to cut 'feed' barley with a foot-engine, sail-reaper or binder, when it was tied into sheaves.

On heavy land, according to Raynbird (1849) 'the barley is mown across the stetches or beds, and when fit to cart, is gathered by the wives of the harvestmen, who use hand rakes for the purpose of rolling the barley off three stetches into a shock, leaving a passage for the waggons in the furrows'. These women, the gavellers, were careful to arrange the barley with the ears all pointing in one direction, facilitating the processes of threshing with the flail and of hummelling to cut off the awns. Loose barley was most often stored in the barn rather than in stacks.

Oats were also gathered loose at one time, but Arthur Young wrote, 'Oats are mown, and gathered loose, as barley. But I have known some very great crops on new land, reaped and bound in sheaves; a practice that ought to be more common'.

A resolution of the Framlingham Farmers' Club, meeting in July 1840, reads: 'Ten sheaves in a shock was the best number. In gavelling barley, the fork was better than the rake. In harvesting beans, the best plan was to use the sickle.'

Later, when mowing was usual for all crops, the scythe was fitted with a cradle, a kind of short rake with teeth up to 18 inches or more, which helped to gather the corn into bundles of the right size for a sheaf. For barley a bale or hoop, sometimes simply a withy cut from the hedge, at others of iron, was used.

Special rates of pay were agreed with the men for getting in the harvest. The general practice during the present century seems to have been to come to terms with the King or Lord of the Harvest (often the head horseman on the farm, according to A. B. Johnson of Kiln Farm, Great Bealings, where he succeeded his father-in-law in 1926), for a fixed sum for getting in the whole harvest. The Lord would negotiate with the other hands, and would be assisted by a second-in-command, known as the Lady. The money was shared out at the end of the harvest, and was in addition to the regular wages. The arrangement was flexible, and the farmer reserved the right to divert labour to other operations. Mr Johnson's father-in-law would include such tasks as chopping out turnips for the sheep, and agree a sum which would enable him to include as many men as possible.

Charles Freeman employed a large number of hands. An entry in his diary for 14th July 1828, reads as follows:

'Hired Harvestmen to give them 7/6 per Acre to cut and clear they to do everything that wants to be done. 6/d. more to be left to me. They to have 1/s. each for Pr. of Gloves their suppers dinner in middle of harvest and 1£ when they have done they to find gavellers when wanted to be paid out of the general fund. Malt as formerly.'

Anyone who has helped to stook a crop profusely laced with thistles will appreciate the reason for the 'Pr. of Gloves'. An allowance of malt and hops, to enable the men to brew their own beer, was customary until well into the present century. On 1st September, 'Harvestmen had their Dinner'.

The account books of W. Rogers, of Boundary Farm, Ilketshall St Margaret, give a very complete picture of harvest arrangements there from 1899 to 1909. The entry for 29th July 1899 is typical: 'C. Barber, H. Catling & N. Saxby agree to get the Harvest in for the sum of £8 each. Thatching and trimming stacks included. I agree to help with all carting do drag-raking & cut Beans with machine.'

At other times the plan of operations is slightly altered. In 1902 the men are 'to mow 26 acres of Wheat and Barley I agree to cut 13 acres of Wheat with Binder & 7 acres of Beans with reaper also help & find a boy to help with carting as much as possible thatching excluded'.

By 1909 the form of agreement has changed; whereas in earlier years the harvest money had in some cases at least specifically included general work, the entry now reads: 'Hammond, Peck and Chapman agree to help to finish up harvest at the sum of 4. 15.—each extra, beside their standing wages.' They also receive 'hireing money of one shilling each.'

Mid-morning saw a break in the work for 'levenses, when the stone beer-jars would be broached. Mid-day brought the wives with more solid provender, and 'someone would always be responsible in seeing that any man whose circumstances at home were such that his women couldn't bring him tea was looked after' (A. B. Johnson). At four o'clock it was time for yet more refreshment—'beevers' in Suffolk.

Many of the old harvest customs described by W. and H. Raynbird (1849) have died out, but A. B. Johnson recalls that of 'shoeing the colt', when an initiate to the harvest field was subjected to the ordeal of having a nail driven into the sole of his boot until, when he could bear it no longer, and cried out, he had to stand a round of ale.

Tusser, in the sixteenth century, tells of extra payment to the Harvest Lord, and the giving of gloves to the reapers, and also the custom of crying largess, when visitors to the harvest-field were expected to donate a shilling.

The last load was decorated with branches, and sometimes flags and streamers. Christopher Ketteridge and Spike Mays (1972), describe the ceremony of the Horkey Bough, when the trace-horse was unhitched from the last load, a rope was attached to his collar and to the bough of an oak, and the latter thus wrenched and torn away, to grace the top of the load. Such a bough still hangs in the great wheat barn at Cressing Temple.*

When all the sheaves had been led away, the ground was raked to take up the loose remnants. Philip Wright (1961) relates how 'my first job in the harvest field . . . . was to drag the iron-toothed rake . . . which for some reason was called the "hobby rake",' to collect what remained. Wooden tines are more usual in the Suffolk hobby rake, or moggy rake; it was often used by a woman, and was later superseded by the horse-rake. Gleaners were not allowed to start work until raking was complete; if the field was to be horse-raked, a single sheaf was left in the centre. The signal to begin was sometimes given by a Queen of the Harvest, or the church bell might be rung for both start and finish.

A. B. Johnson recalls the fashioning of a miniature corn-stack, which was taken into the church at Harvest Festival, and long after the coming of the combine-harvester one sheaf would be cut with the scythe so that it could appear at the Festival in accordance with tradition.

Finally, the end of the harvest was celebrated as adjured by Tusser:

> '*In harvest-time, harvest-folk, servants and all,*
> *should make, all together, good cheer in the hall;*
> *And fill out the black bowle of blythe to their song,*
> *and let them be merry all harvest-time long.*'

This was the Horkey, when the farmer entertained the men and their wives to a supper of roast beef and plum-pudding, washed down by home-brewed beer. According to A. O. D. Claxton (1968), this custom died out at the beginning of the present century, the farmer giving each man one shilling hiring money to buy himself a drink before harvest, and half-a-crown 'frolic money' at the end of harvest, which would be spent jointly with his fellows on a harvest supper at the local. Indeed, as far back as 1813, Charles Freeman wrote in his diary: 'Sept. 2. Harvestment have their frolic at the Pickerel' (a Stowmarket inn).

So much for the corn harvest, but there were other crops to be garnered. Peas

* Scarfe, 1968.

were 'made' (harvested) with a pea-make which, in Arthur Young's words, 'is the half of an old scythe fixed in a handle'. This was no doubt its origin, but a purpose-made implement with a slight S-curve in the blade was found more efficient. The horsedrawn swim-rake, not unlike the hay-sweep, seems to be peculiar to Suffolk. The heavy wooden tines drag up the pea-plants from the ground.

Beans were either pulled by hand by women and children, or 'scrogged' (cut) with a sickle or hook with a strongly curved blade (illustrated by Raynbird).

A. B. Johnson said of mangolds: 'We never stuck a fork into mangolds; they were picked up by hand and thrown into the tumbril.' Beetroot too, whether used as fodder or later grown for sugar-production, must not be pierced and caused to bleed. A root-fork with buttoned tines avoided damage. For lifting, a special blade attachment, made by Ransomes and by Youngs, was fitted to a YL plough body.

Arthur Young records an interesting practice by a farmer of the name of Fuller, who cut out the turnips by cross horse-hoeing, then buried them with a double-tom plough, leaving only the leaf exposed so that the sheep could eat them without getting at the roots. The *Country Gentleman's Catalogue* for 1894 illustrates an iron frame with flat, curved blade, horse-drawn, for uprooting turnips. The Abbot's Hall collection includes a similar implement made by the local blacksmith for Mr Keeble of Brantham Hall.

Potatoes were harvested by means of a plough with feet bearing backward-projecting tines, outspread like fingers, which threw out the potatoes on either side. A later machine carries a pair of spinners at the rear.

Before carting to the stackyard, hay was spread out to dry, and turned from time to time by the hay-toppler or the swath-turner. Hay is light, and the fork used to lift it for loading is long both in shaft and tines compared with the sheaf fork ('shoof-fork' in Suffolk).

Loose barley was often stacked inside the barn, where it was handy for threshing with the flail, but hay and wheat were mostly made into stacks in the open. A staddle or base kept the stack clear of the damp ground, and prevented damage by rats. In East Anglia, where stone is hard to come by, the staddle-stones found in other parts of the country are replaced by iron staddle-pins such as those which supported the rick-stand illustrated by Philip Wright, and used on his father's farm in West Suffolk. Brick stack-bases were used by K. J. Brown of Hill Farm, Framlingham, and William Freeman records the practice of claying-up the sides of the stacks to deter the rats.

In building a stack of corn the sheaves were laid with the ears pointing inward, and so arranged that the centre was higher than the sides, which expanded slightly

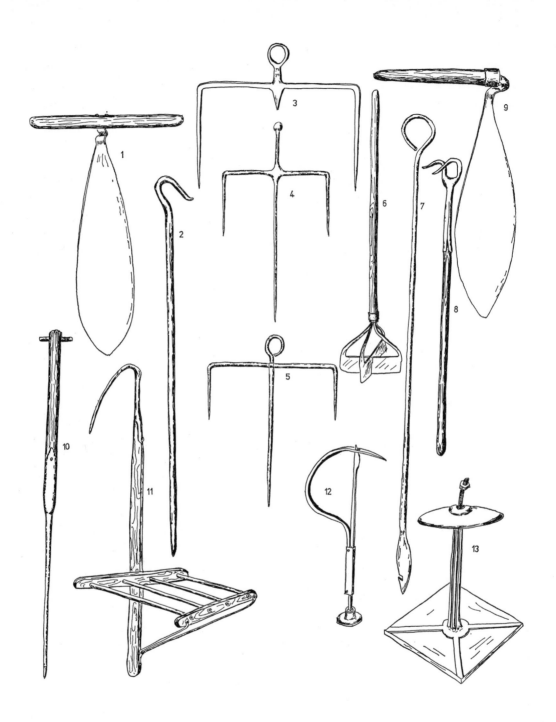

outwards as the height increased, so that the rain would drip off and not penetrate the interior. Further protection was provided by thatching. The ladder was secured by a ladder-hook, which allowed it to be turned over, making it unnecessary to remove the hook every time it was moved along. An earlier form was the stack-pin, which also served as a rest for the yealms of straw. Another form of support for the straw was the stack-cradle; that illustrated came from Ilketshall St Margaret in north Suffolk, but they have been seen in use recently in Essex. The layer of straw forming the thatch was sometimes sewn into a sheet with a stack-needle.

In July 1854 William Freeman was 'making round stack of stover'. His father, when farming in Norfolk in 1820, used the term 'stubber'—'mowing layer [clover] for stubber'. The word is used in Suffolk for hay made from clover (Moor, 1823),* but Tusser writes of 'barley ... Fresh threshed for *stover*', and Ray (1768) gives 'fodder for cattle; straw, or the like. Essex'. Nares' *Classical Glossary* (1822) suggests a derivation from estovers.

The flail was used for threshing here until the mid nineteenth century, and for another hundred years for beans. The threshing floor was specially laid, often of rammed earth, but often of stone or even iron. Philip Wright quotes the Rev. W. L. Rham on the method of construction:

'The soil is taken out to the depth of six to eight inches or more, and if the subsoil is moist a layer of dry sand or gravel is laid at the bottom three or four inches thick, and trod smooth and level. A mixture is made of clay or loam and sand with water to the consistency of common building mortar; to which is added some chalk or pounded shells or gypsum. Chaff, cow-dung and bullock's blood are added and the whole is well worked up together. A coat of this is laid on the prepared bottom with a trowel, about an inch thick and allowed to dry. Another coat is added and the cracks filled up carefully. This is repeated until the required thickness is produced. When it begins to harden, the whole is well-rammed with a heavy wooden rammer and every crack filled up, so as to give it the appearance of a uniform solid body. This is left to harden slowly and in a short time becomes sufficiently hard to be used.

* Pronounced 'stuvver' in Suffolk (*vide* Moor).

Fig. 13. STACKING, ETC.
1. Hay knife, stack knife (with transverse handle). 2. Ladder-hook (thatching). 3, 4, 5. Trussing forks, stack needles. 6. Root chopper. 7. Stack-testing pin. 8. Crome. 9. Stack knife (with lateral handle). 10. Stack-pin (thatching). 11. Stack-cradle (thatching). 12. Stack-thatcher's needle. 13. Staddle-pin (to support stack-base).
(Nos 10 and 11, $\frac{1}{18}$; remainder, $\frac{1}{12}$.)

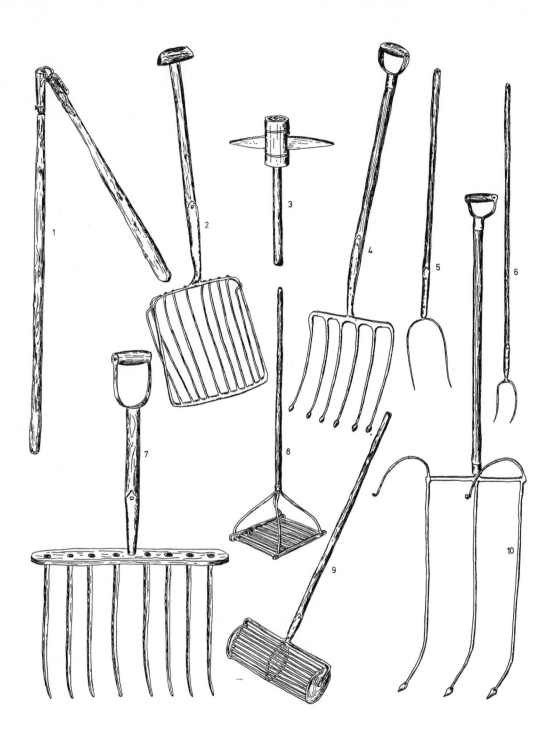

The method of construction of an iron floor has, so far as can be ascertained, never been published, and it is therefore both interesting and valuable to find it given in some detail in the diary of Charles Freeman for 1823. On Thursday, 9th, he is 'carting stone into barn for bottom of Iron floor', and on the 16th, 'Ramming clay down the whole front of barn'. On the 30th, 'Rolled Chalk on barn floor', and on November 5th, 'Rolled Chalk ready to lay Iron upon in barn'.

The threshing floor was laid between the large front and rear doors of the barn in order that the through-draught might speed the process of winnowing to get rid of the chaff.

William Freeman was still hand-threshing both white wheat and oats, and also tares, in the barn in October 1855, although in the same winter he used the horse-engine for barley, and steam-threshing for red and clog wheat. At times he makes it clear that hand-threshing is being used when the grain is wanted for seed.

No precise date seems to be known for the introduction either of the horse-work or of the portable steam-threshing equipment into Suffolk or Essex, although a form of threshing machine had been invented as early as 1827. Ransomes of Ipswich marketed a hand-thresher in 1844, and William Freeman notes on 23rd September 1851 that 'Burrell's steam engine came in the evening', and he used it to thresh barley on the following day; this machine was made by Chas. Burrell of Ixworth. The earliest reference to the use of the horse-work in the diaries is January 1852, when it was used for clover.

The flail ('stick-and-a-half' in Suffolk) consisted of a hand-staff, usually of ash, some 4 or 5 feet in length, to which was attached a swingle of blackthorn or other tough wood, 3 feet long. The joint varied in form, but typically comprised a swivel formed by bending a strip of green ash to form a cap over the knobbed end of the hand-staff; this was lashed to the swingle by a strip of eel-skin (or sometimes oxhide). Two layers of corn were laid with the ears facing inwards. Two men facing each other would swing their flails alternately in rhythm, the chaff being carried away by the draught blowing through the open doors of the barn. The grain was next gathered up, using the scuppit, a broad shovel often made from one piece of willow, and sieved to get rid of the chaff. Later a corn-dresser, with a combination of rotating vanes and oscillating screens, was used.

Barley created a special problem. Threshing with the flail did not remove the

Fig. 14. THRESHING
1. Flail (stick-and-a-half in Suffolk). 2. Root shovel. 3. Mill-bill and thrift. 4. Beet fork. 5. Hay fork. 6. Sheaf fork, shoof fork. 7. Cavings fork (an early wooden form). 8. Barley hummeler, haveller (grid type). 9. Hummeler (rotary type). 10. Cavings fork.
(No. 1, $\frac{1}{8}$; 5 and 6, $\frac{1}{24}$; remainder, $\frac{1}{12}$.)

awn, the sharp spike at the tip of each grain, and an implement known as a hummeler or haveller was used for this purpose. Various forms are known; a square or rectangular head of iron may have either fixed or movable blades, or a closely set grid of intersecting blades; or the implement may take the form of a roller, or twin rollers, with parallel blades to cut off the awns.

Several local firms made threshing machines, perhaps the most notable being Garretts of Leiston, who also manufactured the portable engines by which they were powered. The development of this firm is yet another example of great expansion from small beginnings. The founder, Richard Garrett, was the son of a smith whose speciality was the making of sickles. Richard started in business by first hiring and then purchasing a forge when he was still only twenty-one years of age, in 1798.

Both at the time of the portable engine, which had to be horse-drawn from farm to farm, and later when the engines were self-propelled, it was the usual practice for farmers to engage the services of a contractor, and here the custom differed as between Suffolk and Essex. In the latter county, a full crew would accompany and operate the machine, whilst in Suffolk only two or three men would be sent, the farmer finding the rest from his own men or calling in loose hands; as the machine progressed round the district, local farmers would co-operate by making men available.

In 1906 W. P. Rogers hired five extra men at 2s. 6d. each and a boy at 1s. 6d., the men receiving board-money of 4s. for the five. The men's wages had risen to 3s. in 1907, but they had to perform other tasks such as chaff-cutting. In 1897 he paid £5. 3. 6 for threshing 276 coombs of wheat, barley, oats, beans and peas. From 1906 the account is presented in a new form, giving a breakdown showing variety and amount, the number of hours of employment of the cutter and of the pitcher, and so forth, and this would seem to imply that more labour is being supplied by the contractor.

Whilst still in the stack, both hay and corn had to be carefully watched for signs of overheating, and for this purpose a long steel rod, with a barbed point, was used to sample the centre of the stack. A neat version of this instrument, in three detachable sections which fitted into a leather sheath, was also employed for sampling the quality of the hay or corn when buying it in the stack.

Hay was cut for fodder with a heavy and cumbersome knife, and the truss separated by means of the trussing fork or hay-needle, generally a three-pronged instrument with two short outer prongs and a long centre one; an example with centre prong shorter than the others was said to be used for clover.

As in the harvest field, so in the stackyard, the scene is less picturesque than of yore, the stacks repeating the geometric pattern of the bales of which they are formed. But the old methods still prevail when the straw is needed for thatching, so once again the long-straw wheat of earlier days is grown, cut with the binder and threshed in the drum.

'Goof' or 'goaf' in Suffolk, 'goffe' in Essex, is the term given by Moor for corn stacked in the barn, and the word is of ancient vintage, for Tusser uses it, or rather the verb derived from it:

> '*In goving at harvest learn skilfully how*
> *Each grain for to lay by itself on the mow:*
> *Seed barley the purest gove out of the way,*
> *All other nigh hand, just gove as ye may.*'

A gofe-ladder, listed by Tusser amongst the barn implements in his *Digression to Husbandly Furniture*, used as the stack grew higher, was still known in Moor's time.

The stack had to be trodden down as it rose, and for this purpose a horse was brought in, ridden by a lad—'riding the goof'. When the time came for it to descend to earth, a rope was tied to its tail and it was eased down.

The earliest form of chaff-cutter was the chaff-box, with a blade working guillotine-fashion as the straw was pushed to the end of the box. Wheel-operated chaff-cutters were, however, common at least from the early part of the nineteenth century. Charlie Brundish had one on Tan Office Farm, made by Garrood of Eye in 1840; it needed two men to operate it. Like his corn-dresser, manufactured by Bewley of Stowmarket in 1839 and kept in use until 1963, it must have served his grandfather and father before him.

6 Markets, Men and Mills

The prices realized for corn and other products fluctuated greatly. The Freeman diaries show wheat fetching 30s. per coomb in January 1821, with barley at 12s. 6d.; in April 1822 wheat was down to 21s., barley 9s., and beans 10s., though wheat reached 24s. in June of that year. This was a considerable drop from the returns in 1820, when white wheat was sold for 40s. and red for 35s., but in 1851 prices had declined still further, the 'top price of good red wheat 18/6', though barley brought some compensation at 12s. 9d. Prices for 1854 were picking up— wheat at 36s., barley 18s. and new beans at 25s.

This hardly seems to confirm the oft-repeated statement that the labourer's wage was the price of a coomb of wheat. Charlie Brundish, recorded on tape a few years ago, had this to say about prices in his father's time, c. 1900: 'If you made thirteen to fourteen shillin' a coomb of wheat, that would be about the outside; you'd want a good sample of wheat to make, say, about sixteen or seventeen shillin'. My father always told me, "A coomb o' wheat should pay a man a week".'

A Mr Cooper of Blythburgh Lodge, Suffolk, quoted by Raynbird, took the average price of wheat as his standard 'both as being the most valuable production of the labourer's toil, and the principal article of his food'. He paid 8s. per week when wheat was above 5s. per bushel and under 6s., increasing the wage by 1s. for every shilling in the price of wheat. He also had an arrangement with the miller to supply his labourers at cost price.

In 1905 W. P. Rogers was paying his men according to the number of days worked, according to his valuation of the worth of each man's work. For six days, Earl got 14s., Barber 12s. and Collyer 8s. 6d., with overtime at the rate of 3d., 2d., or 1d. By 1941 he was paying only £2. 8. 0. less insurance, then 1s. 2½d.

Charlie Hill of Snape began work in 1905, at the age of thirteen, on a wage of 3s. 6d. a week, helping the cowman; four years later, the latter hanged himself, so Charlie succeeded, at a man's wage of 14s. at the age of seventeen. It was customary to make promotion, which usually came at twenty-one, conditional on the ability to lift a sack of wheat on to the wagon; Charlie was capable of this, and got the job.

At a time when the unions are pressing for a weekly wage of £50, these figures must seem incredible, on looking back, to those who earned them.

The mills that ground the corn were of four main types (Pls 61–3), of which three —tower mill, smock mill and post mill—harnessed the power of the wind to turn the stones; the fourth was the watermill, probably the first to be introduced to this country. Other sources of power were in fact used; one mill, of which a fuller account will be given later, started as a horse-driven mill, was converted to a smock mill and was eventually powered by an engine.

The process by which the natural forces are harnessed to provide power for the machinery of the mill, whether wind or water, is complicated, but an outline of the working of a windmill will serve to explain the general principle involved. The wind, striking the sails of the windmill, causes them to rotate in a vertical plane, and this motion is conveyed through the main shaft to the brake wheel, the cogs of which engage with those of a horizontal wheel, or gear, the wallower, which is mounted on the centre-post and causes it to rotate; the motion is passed on through the spur-wheel, mounted at the lower end of the centre-post, to the stone-nuts, or gears, which effect the rotation of the upper mill stones. A subsidiary arrangement of gears controls the hoists and operates smaller machines for oat-crushing, kibbling barley, peas and other crops.

The sails may have canvas covers which can be reefed and thus adjusted to the force of the wind, or slats which can be opened or closed like those of a venetian blind, or a combination of both, as is the case with the Drinkstone post mill.

In the case of the post mill, the whole body of the mill, machinery and all, is set on the top of a post supported by a structure of cross-beams. In most cases the frame was later enclosed in a 'round-house', which also served for storage. The mill had to be rotated into the wind; this was formerly done by hand, but a fantail with miniature sails was generally added later.

In both tower mill and smock mill the machinery is housed in the fixed body, and only the cap rotates; the tower mill is brick-built, the smock mill timbered.

The principle in the watermill is the same, substituting water for wind and wheel for sails. A variant of the watermill is the tide-mill, which of course could operate only in tidal waters; a mill-pool filled as the tide rose, and flowed through the mill at ebb tide.

Watermills may be undershot or overshot, that is, the water may flow under the wheel or fall on it from above; the latter method is considered much more effective.

In many cases windmills and watermills operated in pairs, to allow for the vagaries of the weather. This was especially so in the case of the Essex tide-mills, of which at one time there were seven; the tide-mill at Woodbridge in Suffolk has been recently restored. Another frequent combination was that of mill and farm.

A group of particular interest is that at Drinkstone, where the history of the mills is bound up with that of the family in whose ownership they have remained for over two hundred years. Wilfred Clover's great-great-great-grandfather bought the post mill, built in 1689, in the year 1760; it was then a true post mill supported by a frame of cross-trees and struts. His great-grandfather added the round-house, inside which the original cross-trees may be seen overhead. The mill was turned into the wind by means of a long tail-beam, at first by sheer manual effort, but later supported by a wheel running in a track. Later still a fantail, or fly, was added, so that turning into the wind was automatic; dismantled mills supplied the gear —the fly-post from Woolpit and the fan from Stradbroke.

The mill has two pairs of sails, one pair spring-operated, the other of the older 'common' type with canvases, entailing the tiresome and at times hazardous task of reefing. There are also two pairs of stones—head and tail according to their position in relation to the orientation of the mill. At one time stones of Millstone Grit from the Peak District of Derbyshire were commonly used in Suffolk, but later gave way to the French Burr stone, which gave a finer grind. Some mills used both—Grit for animal feeding stuffs, barley, etc., and French Burr for flour, but for many years the Drinkstone mill has used only Burr stones. The slabs are not of sufficient size to make whole stones; the blocks are arranged and bound together in iron collars. In dressing Grit with the mill-bill comparatively coarse furrows are cut; the Burr stones have a series of finer intermediate channels.

Mr Clover joined his father on leaving school in 1922. At times they would work from 6.30 or 7 a.m. until 10 or 11 o'clock at night; advantage had to be taken of the wind. 'We never thought we'd done a day's work if we knocked off before 10 o'clock at night, those days.' For light, candles were used. 'If you accidentally knock a candle over, it goes out; an oil lamp burns and sets alight.'

The smock mill began as a 'round-house', if a building with sixteen sides warrants that description. A horse turned the shaft, which operated the stones in the chamber above. In the time of Mr. Clover's great-great-grandfather it was converted into a smock mill by the addition of an upper structure of eight sides, and sails. At this stage it was found that a large tree on the land of a neighbouring farmer literally 'took the wind out of the sails', and one dark night this was remedied by ring-barking the tree, which duly withered and died, and was cut

68. *Mole-draining horse-gin, showing method of operation. From Henry Stephen's* Book of the Farm, *4th edn., Division VI (1888).*

69. *Mole-draining horse-gin, c. 1820, from Wimbish.*

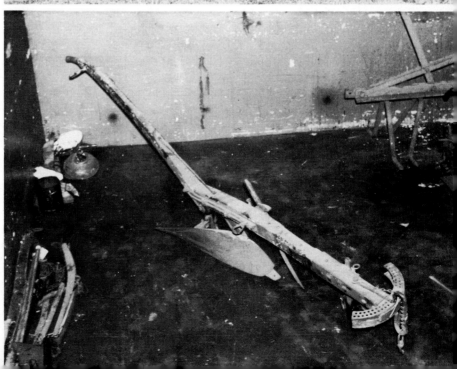

70. *Ransomes' AY Plough (1835), with single stilt with peg to aid turning.*

71. *George Turner (in rear) using an AY plough made by Bendall of Woodbridge; Dial Farm, Earl Soham, 1905.*

72. *Ransomes' YL plough fitted with bowl-wheel ('pudden-wheel') and side-bracket.*

73. *Ploughing with a Cornish and Lloyds' GCB wooden swing plough with detachable second stilt, at Hintlesham.*

74. *Ploughing with a Ransomes' YL iron plough (1844) and a pair of Suffolks, c. 1900.*

75. *A rib-roll at Bushes Farm, Haughley.*

76. *Carting manure; the 'toe-bar' of the left-hand tumbril can be seen, as can the difference between the harness of the shaft-horse and trace-horse.*

95. A horsework (horse-gear) operating the elevator at Goodchild's farm, Little Wenham.

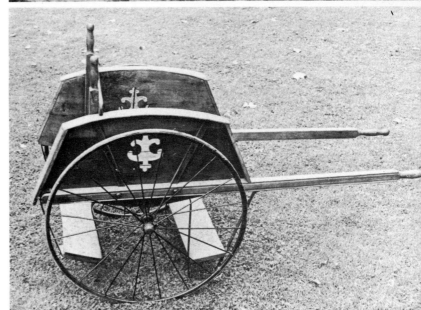

96. A gleaning cart; the child can be taken out to the field, and the sheaf tied on to the back, or a second child perch on the step.

97. Stooking wheat cut by the tractor-drawn binder, 18th August 1961.

98. *Threshing with the flail at Oakley, Essex.*

99. *A corn-dresser; turning the handle revolves the vanes, creating draught, and activates the gridded trays.*

100. *Steam threshing at Hill Farm, Iken, c. 1890; a watercart stands by to replenish the boiler of the engine.*

101. *Pea-harvesting at Kenton, 1887; the men are using 'pea-makes'.*

102. *Using the turnip-pick to lift turnips after sheep have been feeding.*

103. *Turnip-lifter; made by the local blacksmith for Mr Keeble of Brantham Hall.*

104. Potato plough; the feet uproot and spread the potatoes.

105. Potato-digger (spinner); rotating forks at the rear throw out the potatoes.

106. Wooden-framed beet-lifter; used by Joe Stearn of Onehouse Hall.

107. Beet-plough; the angle of the blades is adjustable.

108. The Women's Land Army of 1916; pulling flax at Mendlesham.

109. 'Beevers' or 'fourses' at Culpho Hall Farm, c. 1908. This photograph, taken by Mr G. P. Watkins, who farmed Culpho Hall Farm at the time, is of particular interest as demonstrating the relation of staffing to acreage. Culpho Hall had an extent of rather less than 150 acres. Mr A. B. Johnson has supplied the following notes on those shown in the photograph:

1. Joe Kidby, head cowman. 2. Connie Worth, daughter of head man. 3. Mrs John Goodchild, wife of second horseman. 4. A young daughter of Mrs Goodchild. 5. Charlie Worth ('Ruffie'), head horseman; respected by master and man alike. 6. Harold Kidby, son of Joe. 7. Percy Worth, third horseman, son of Ruffie, known as 'Stormer', on account of his rather quick temper. 8. Olly Kidby, another son of Joe, backhouse and poultry boy. 9. Hawes, a labourer from Grundisburgh. 10. Sam Church, pigman and expert drainer (see Pl. 59). 11. Mrs Chas. Worth, wife of head horseman. 12. Ethel Goodchild, daughter of John Goodchild. 13. Maggie Church, daughter of Sam; she kept house for him, as he was a widower. 14. Peter Girling, labourer: walked daily from Tuddenham (1½m.) to work as regularly as clockwork; generally loaded with kindling on way home. 15. Billy Smy, labourer; oldest man on farm; so loved as he grew older that others would share his load. 16. Walter Green, horseman at Abbey Farm; very steady, some would have said, slow.

110. *A sheep-shearing gang at Foxhall, near Ipswich.*

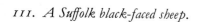

111. *A Suffolk black-faced sheep.*

112. *Shepherd Brown, of New-bourne.*

down by its unsuspecting owner. The machinery was subsequently dismantled, and fresh stones powered by an engine were installed.

The introduction of steam-powered mills and later the roller mills in the towns reduced the local mills to the grinding of barley and beans for pig and poultry food, although at least one miller, Reuben Rackham of Wickham Market, added a steam-powered rolling-mill as an auxiliary to his watermill in 1893. The engine was made by the firm of Whitmore and Binyon, also of Wickham Market, and is now at the Abbot's Hall Museum; the rolling-mill is at the Bridewell Museum in Norwich.

At Drinkstone the cost to the farmer of grinding a coomb of wheat, before the 1914–18 war, was 1s. 6d.

Mills did more than perform the function for which they were built; they were, and in some cases remain, an integral part of the rural scene, the watermill quietly enhancing the charm of the stream, the windmill more flamboyantly breaking the skyline. Cobbett, in the course of his *Rural Rides* in 1829, viewing them from Ipswich, thought them 'the most beautiful sight of the kind that I have ever beheld'. He counted 'in the vicinage ... no less than seventeen. They are all painted or washed white; the sails are black; it was a fine morning, the wind was brisk, and their twirling altogether, added greatly to the beauty of the scene'.

It is good to know that efforts are being made to preserve those that are left, and with the present problems of power it may be well not to lose all knowledge of this source.

Some farms installed a small stone-mill in the end of a barn, and ground meal for animal feeding, using horse-work, steam-engine or tractor, geared through a hole cut in the wall. Such a mill, from a farm at Henley, awaits re-assembly at the Abbot's Hall Museum.

It was not unknown for windmills to be transported for quite long distances; this was especially the case with timber-framed mills. Round about 1840 the post mill at Wingfield was moved to Syleham, not a far cry, and in 1845 a mill formerly standing on the castle mound at Eye was found a new site at Cranley. A smock-mill formerly at Cransford was re-erected at Peasenhall, some five miles away. In or about 1880, the greatest feat in terms of distance was achieved by the removal of a post mill from Yarmouth in Norfolk to Crowfield in Suffolk, a journey of over forty miles, and in 1886 the mill at Weybread was moved to Framsden, where it stood only about a hundred yards from the existing post mill.

No doubt the venture was regarded as worthwhile; dismantling and re-erection were helped by the practice, in timbered mills as in houses, of numbering the beams before building in the first place.

7 Livestock

HORSES

Until the coming of the motor car and the railway, the horse provided the principal means of transport, whether ridden or driven. On the farm its period of usefulness was even longer, and the crowded streets of London can still provide the sight of a brewer's dray drawn by a team of heavy shires.

In Suffolk and Essex, however, it is the Suffolk Punch which has dominated the scene, although Shires, Clydesdales, Percherons and crosses of these have pulled the plough, particularly in Essex, and still do so on the occasion of the annual drawing matches.

P. J. O. Trist (1971) states that '*Camden's Britannia* gives the date of the Suffolk as far back as 1506', but the identity of this horse with the Suffolk of recent years must remain uncertain. A definitive account of the breed was published in 1880 by the Suffolk Horse Society in the first volume of its stud-book. It was written by Herman Biddell, a member of a farming family at Playford, near Ipswich, whose apologies for its imperfections may be written off as becoming but unjustified modesty.

Biddell enumerates the points which go to make the true Suffolk; there is an insistence on the maintenance of the traditional colour, a range of seven shades of *chesnut*; the muscular shoulder, the deep carcase which

'is, or should be, a *sine-qua-non* with a Suffolk horse. The long hours without food, which seems a rooted practice all over the county, render a roomy carcase a positive necessity. A Clydesdale or Shire-bred with a light middle and short rib may do in London, where the nose-bag is always at hand, but the long day, and short rations, from 6–30 to 3–0 o'clock on the plough in Suffolk would soon reduce a horse of this form to a skeleton'.

The old breed had its defects, in particular the feet, which were said to be 'brittle and otherwise defective', but these disabilities were overcome by judicious cross-

? domestication

breeding, which was accomplished without losing the characteristics that have made the horse famous.

Our earliest sources of information come from Arthur Young and other writers of his time. In 1770 he visited the whole of the eastern area, and the results were published in his *Farmer's Tour Through the East of England* (1771) in which he writes:

'The breed of horses peculiar to this county is one of the greatest curiosities in it; I never yet saw anything that are comparable to them in shape, or the amazing power they have in drawing. They are called the sorrel breed, the colour a bay sorrel; the form that of a true round barrel, remarkably short, and the legs the same, and lower over the forehead than in any part of the back, which they reckon here a point of consequence. They sell at surprising rates: the good geldings and mares at from 35 to 60 guineas each, and small ones of 8, 9 or 10 years old at 20l., but none of them are very large. The work they will do is extraordinary being beyond comparison stronger and hardier than any of the great black breeds of Flanders, Northamptonshire or Yorkshire. They are all taught with very great care to draw in concert, and many farmers are so attentive to this point that they will have teams, every horse of which will fall on his knees at the word of command twenty times running in the full drawing attitude, and all at the same moment, but without exerting any strength, till a variation of the word orders them to give all their strength, and then they will carry out amazing weights. It is common to draw team against team for high wagers. It was considered by many people here that 4 good horses in a narrow-wheeled waggon would, without any hurt or mischief from over-working, carry 30 sacks of wheat, each 4 bushels (near 9 gallons measure), 30 miles, if proper fair time was given them. A waggon weighs about 25 cwt; this weight, therefore, is very near 5 tons and, let me add, they have not a turnpike near them. One might venture to assert that there are not 4 great black horses in England would do this.'

In 1797 Young is less complimentary about the horses's appearance, though not of its performance:

'In some respects, an uglier horse could not be viewed; sorrel colour, very low in the fore-end, a large ill-shaped head, with slouching heavy ears, a great carcass and short legs, but short-backed, and more of the *punch* than the Leicestershire breeders will allow. These horses could only walk and draw; they could trot no better than a cow. But their power in drawing was very considerable. Of late years, by aiming at coach horses, the breed is much changed to a handsomer, lighter, and more active horse.'

The intention was to use them as carriage-horses as well as for agricultural work. Jery Cullum, in a footnote to Young's description, has the following to say: 'Clean legs and well-found shoulders are criterions of the true Suffolk horse, points which entitle them to be good movers; and such they are in general, if used in chaises, and not too long habituated to draw only', and Sir Thomas Cullum of Hawstead wrote in 1780:

'Suffolk punch horse is of a remarkably short and compact make, and generally about 15 hands high, their legs bony, and their shoulders loaded with flesh. They are not made to indulge the rapid impatience of this posting generation, but for draught they are perhaps as unrivalled as for their gentle and tractable temper. Though natives of a province varied with only the slightest inequalities of surface, yet when arrived into mountainous regions they seem born for that service. With wonder and gratitude have I seen them with the most spirited exertions, unsolicited by the whip and indignant as it were at the obstacles that opposed them, drawing my carriage up the rocky and precipitous road of Denbigh and Carnarvonshire.'

Drawing matches (not to be confused with the ploughing trials now commonly advertised under that title) were a popular test of strength and endurance, a public spectacle, and an opportunity to indulge the universal weakness for gambling. Herman Biddell gives an account of a match held in 1742; another is given by Raynbird (1849), who quotes an advertisement appearing in the *Suffolk Mercury* of 22nd June 1724:

'On Thursday, 9th., July, 1724, there will be a drawing at Ixworth Pickarel, for a piece of plate of 45*s*. value; and they that will bring five horses or mares may put in for it, and they that draw 20 the best and fairest pulls, with their reins up; and they that carry the greatest weight over the block with fewest lifts and fewest pulls shall have the said plate, by such judges as the masters of the teams shall choose. You are to meet at 12 o'clock, and put in your names, or else be debarred from drawing for it and subscribe half-a-crown a piece to be paid to the second-best team.'

Fig. 15. ANIMAL CARE
1. Shepherd's crook. 2. Docking iron. 3. Singeing lamp. 4, 5, 6, 7. Bull-holders (locally humbug, barnacles). 8. Cow-yoke. 9. Mane and tail comb. 10. Lamb crook. 11. Sweat scraper. 12. Bit (double-snaffle). 13. Pendant-bit. 14. Box-bit. 15. Horn-cups (to control growth). 16, 17. Hoof-picks. 18. Harness-rack. 19. Horse-boot, lawn-boot. 20. Horse-boot for Suffolk horse. 21. Horse-boot for Shire horse. 22. Cattle-cradle (to prevent self-suckling). 23. Sweat scraper.
(Nos. 1, 8, 10, 18 and 22, $\frac{1}{12}$; remainder, $\frac{1}{16}$.)

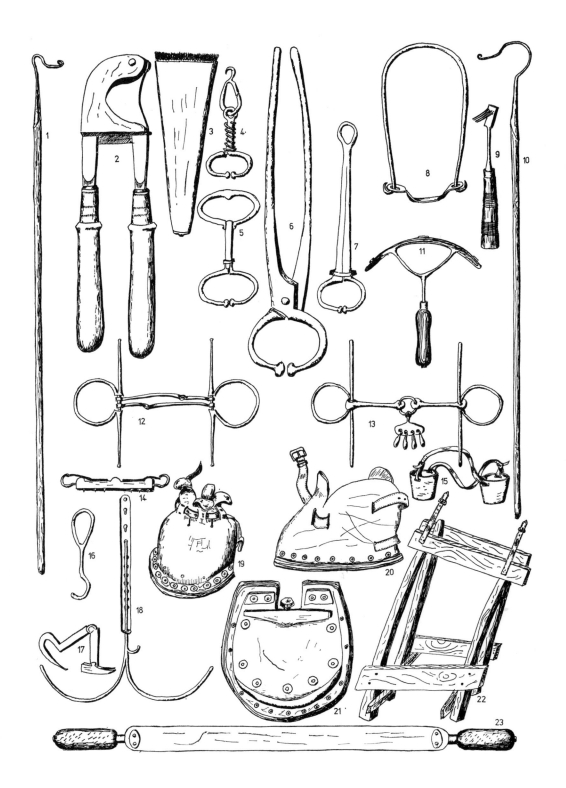

Raynbird goes on to describe the nature of the contest:

'The trial was made with a waggon loaded with sand, the wheels sunk a little into the ground with blocks of wood laid before them to increase the difficulty. The first efforts are made with the reins fastened as usual to the collar; but the animals cannot when so confined put out their whole strength; the reins are therefore afterwards thrown loose on their necks when they exert their utmost powers, which they usually do by falling on their knees and drawing in that attitude. That they may not break their knees by this operation, the area on which they draw is strewn with soft sand.'

Virtually all the Suffolk horses appearing in the stud-book are descended in the male line from one horse, that of Thomas Crisp of Ufford, foaled in 1768, and advertised in 1773, 'at a fee of eight shillings, as a sire for good stock for coach or road.'

But it was not only for its drawing power that the Suffolk horse compared favourably with other breeds; Hector Moore, farrier, tells of the difficulties he encountered when shoeing Shire horses—'a wonderful horse, but completely useless in this area . . . they got these dreadful leg infections; they would swell, and burst out all pus and matter and then there'd be big growths like bunches of grapes, and when you used to put the shoe on, and the smoke got in amongst it, the maggots would come out . . . that's all tied up with the lime content in the soil.'

The other great horse industry, centred on Newmarket and associated with the racing for which that town is famous, is of course the rearing of bloodstock; many winners of the classics have been foaled in Newmarket stables.

Some of the equipment associated with the horse is illustrated here, and detailed descriptions need not be given, but some items are worthy of special mention.

Horse-boots, or *lawn-boots* as they were called by Harry Loveday Ulph, the Essex saddler, were worn to protect the turf from the iron shoes when the horse drew the mower or roller. Sweat scrapers call to mind the *strigil* used by the Roman after taking his bath; hand-clippers were in common use, but a mechanical clipper on a stand, the cutting head worked by a cable similar to that which operates the speedometer of a car, needed two men for its use.

The words of command used by the horseman are difficult to represent with any degree of accuracy in print; they differ radically from any outside East Anglia. Perhaps the nearest rendering is 'cup-ee-wheesh' for a turn to the left or, according to Claxton, merely 'cup-e'; for a right turn, 'wheesh', or once again quoting Claxton, 'wurr-de-whish' or 'whish' or 'wurr-de'.

CATTLE

Raynbird (1849) quotes Camden's *Britannia* as evidence that Suffolk has been noted for its dairy cattle for more than 250 years. It is certain that the Suffolk Dun, as it was earlier known, has a long history. John C. Morton's *Cyclopaedia of Agriculture* (1855) says:

'It is a polled breed, of which the prevailing colour formerly was a mouse dun, which has changed latterly to pale red.' Arthur Young says that 'the breed is universally polled', but qualifies this in a footnote by stating that 'a certain proportion of the calves would have horns, if reared: the inconvenience of horned cattle among horses, and the damage they do to fences, are an inducement to the farmers to sell all the calves as veal to the butchers, or to the sucklers, which would have horns, and to keep for stock only the polled ones. The horns are to be felt at a very early age.'

In view of later developments, and the failure of the effort to establish the Red Poll as a dual-purpose animal, Morton's comment on the relative merits of polled cattle and shorthorns is of interest, coming as it does a hundred years earlier.

'These cattel are ungainly in their form, and of little value to the grazier, but possess an undoubted capacity of yielding a large quantity of milk, in proportion to the food which they consume. But here, also, the superiority of the short-horns, for the combined purposes of the dairy and the fattening stall, is acknowledged; and indications given that they are, by and by, to supplant the native breed.'

Concerning form, Young states that 'the points admitted are, a clean throat, with little dewlap; a snake head; clean thin legs, and short; a springing rib, and large carcass; a flat loin, the hip bones to lie square and even; the tail to rise high from the rump'.

In Norfolk, a strain of polled cattle was also in course of development, and Trist records that in 1873 breeders from both counties met to draft a 'Standard Description', published in the Index volume of the herd book of 1882, and in the following year the designation of 'Red Polled' was adopted, omitting the county designations. Trist also quoted the re-drafted description of 1939 as follows:

'The Red Poll is a dual purpose animal. The breed was evolved to combine the production of the very highest standard beef with a satisfactory milk yield. Accordingly, judging should aim at deciding the best combination of these qualities. Moreover, an obvious deficiency in one cannot be counterbalanced by superlative excellence in the other.'

The popularity of the breed spread throughout the country, but its very popularity, coupled with the post-war boom in pedigree cattle, was to some extent its undoing, as quality did not keep pace with quantity. In 1959 and 1960, delegates from the Red Poll Society visited several countries with strong cattle-breeding associations, and it was decided to try to enhance the properties of the Red Poll breed by a cross with the Danish Red cattle. Under licence, 87 maiden heifers and 6 bulls were imported, and although some success was achieved, the Friesian has of late years tended more and more to displace the local breed.

In the days before mechanization, cattle had other uses than the production of milk and beef. Oxen, large, powerful and heavily horned, were often used in place of, or in addition to, horses, to draw ploughs, harrows and other implements.

As with horses, so with cattle; the problems of their care were met with the countryman's usual inventiveness. The cow with a tendency to suckle itself was strapped into a 'cradle' of wood which fitted over the withers, preventing the head from turning sufficiently to allow this misdemeanour; a double version of the iron cow-yoke served the same purpose. Another device was a collar with sharp spikes which caused enough discomfort to act as a deterrent. A similar, smaller collar placed round the neck of a calf helped in weaning.

The bull had a ring fitted through the cartilage of the nose, which was punched for the purpose. The bull-leader, a rod with a spring clip for attachment to the ring, allowed the bull to be kept at a distance. The bull-holder (sometimes locally miscalled a bull-leader) was a short tongs-like instrument with rounded tips to the jaws, used to grip the nostrils; when closed it was secured by a sliding clip, or a spring. Local names, 'barnacles' and 'humbug', are used in different areas (see Fig. 15).

In July 1865 disaster in the form of a cattle plague struck Suffolk. A total of 2,498 animals died on 354 farms, a loss of nearly five per cent of existing stock. Special insurance policies were issued, and so alarmed were the local populace that services of intercession were held in the churches. In a hymn specially composed for the occasion the Almighty was petitioned, somewhat naïvely, to grant 'that our sheep may bring forth thousands and ten thousands *in our streets*.* That our oxen strong to labour may not know nor fear decay'.

Although the disease affected mostly cattle, sheep were not immune, as the hymn implies. The severity of the onslaught can be judged by the figures for

* The italics are mine.

individual farms:* forty-eight out of sixty on a farm at Lakenheath; at Bardwell, forty-two were attacked, and eleven slaughtered healthy; at West Row the whole stock of forty-one were attacked by the disease.

SHEEP

It was not until 1859 that Suffolk sheep were given recognition as a separate breed, although Arthur Young says that 'the Norfolk breed of sheep spread over almost every part of the county' [Suffolk]; and as the most famous flocks are about Bury (much more celebrated than any in Norfolk), it has been observed, that they ought rather to be called the Suffolk breed'. Among their 'principal excellencies' he notes 'the quality of the mutton; it being admitted at Smithfield, that as long as the cool weather lasts, it has, for the table of the curious, no superior in texture or grain, flavour, quantity and colour of gravy, with fat enough for such tables. In tallow, they reckon no sheep better. . . . The wool is fine, being in price, per pound, the third sort in England'.

Raynbird (1849), speaking of the flocks kept on the light land of Suffolk, said that they were 'generally Down ewes (black faces), a little cross with the Norfolk, to increase their size, with a Leicester tup; thus getting lambs of good size. Good quality of wool, and with aptitude to fatten'. He recorded the introduction at Chillesford of Cotswold tups with good results, and there were 'many flocks of celebrity of pure Downs, a few Leicester flocks, and still fewer real Norfolk flocks'. So it would appear that although the Suffolk breed is generally accepted as a derivative of the Norfolk horned breed crossed with the Southdown, other factors have gone into the making of it. The black face is no doubt a Southdown characteristic, and the horns have been lost in the process of crossing.

Turnips were the staple diet, and grazing in the field was general, at first at all events, especially for breeding ewes; some farmers cut a proportion of the crop first for cattle feed before turning on the ewes. The method noted elsewhere, of covering the roots by ploughing, leaving only the tops exposed for grazing, does not seem to have been much followed in Suffolk and Essex, though Raynbird tells of the practice of

'laying three drills in a furrow; two rows of turnips are first pulled and laid on one side to give passage for the plough, a furrow is drawn, and three drills of turnips

* Given in *British Parliamentary Papers*, 1867–8, XVIII, p. 239, being Appendix No. 1 of 'A Report on the Cattle Plague in Great Britain during the years 1865, 1866, and 1867', quoted by Thirsk and Imray, 1958.

laid with their tops to the land side; they are now covered by the first-ploughed furrow being turned back. When wanted for use the turnips are thrown out by running a plough along the furrow.'

The method was used for both white turnips and swedes, and had the advantage that pulling the turnips checked the growth of the stems, which drew on the store of nutriment in the soil.

Chaff cut from the straw of oats, wheat, peas or clover, together with hay, was mixed with seed-cake.

Shearing was carried out by a skilled team. In order to foster this skill the West Suffolk Agricultural Association (founded in 1833, amalgamated with East Suffolk in 1856) offered prizes at an annual competition. Each candidate had to shear 4 hoggetts—2 Southdowns and 2 half-breeds—between the hours of 10 and 1.0. The prizes were First: £2; Second: £1. 10s.; Third: £1; Fourth: 15s.; Fifth: 10s. Of the unsuccessful candidates, the five best received 5s. each, the next five 2s. 6d., and the remainder of the contestants 1s. So there were no losers!

The shepherd's crook was made by the blacksmith, though inevitably in time it was produced commercially. There were two kinds; the familiar type with the narrow loop designed to catch the errant sheep by the leg, and one with a wider loop which would take the lamb by the throat; its leg might be broken by the use of the narrow crook (see Fig. 15). Shears were the same for shearer or thatcher, but a clipping machine similar in essence to that used for the horse could be operated by two men.

PIGS

The principal breeds in Suffolk and Essex seem to have been originally quite distinct, but eventually crosses between these and other breeds eliminated county divisions.

Arthur Young, in his survey of agriculture in Essex (1807), quotes another authority in recommending a cross with the Chinese,* 'the most hardy and best qualified to *prog* for themselves'. Of Suffolk, he says only 'that the short white breed of the cow district has very great merit: well made, thick short noses, small bone, and light offals; but not quite so prolific as some worse made breeds'.

A Mr Western of Felix Hall, Essex, at that time reputed to be by far the best

---

* Raynbird (1849) says: 'The Suffolk hog shows its half-Chinese descent in its upright ears, dish face, and pendent belly.'

breeder of pigs, had developed a strain which was described as follows: 'They are black and white, short hair, fine skin, little prick ears, short snubby noses, very fine bone, broad, deep, straight, and light in the belly; full in the hindquarters; and bring litters from eight to twelve'. He designated these the 'Essex half-black'.

It was in Essex that the earliest attempts were made to keep pigs in a clean and orderly fashion. Mr Pattison of Maldon is recorded by Young as having introduced the practice of 'fatting large hogs in separate stalls, so constructed that the animal can, at his pleasure, conveniently rise up and lay down, but cannot turn round'. The base of each stall was sloped from front to back, to avoid fouling. They were fed with barley meal mixed with water. Mr Wakefield of Burnham had pigs from Mr Western, and took things a stage further. He found that when the half-blacks were fed on clover, the white parts of the skin were apt to crack; and by selection he produced an all-black strain.

Sir Richard Neave, of Dagnam Park, was of a more frugal disposition; he grew potatoes, which he boiled, and mixed with biscuit-makers' sweepings!

In course of time, Suffolk became dominant in the sphere of pig-breeding in the whole of the country, and in 1910 a group of farmers founded the St Edmund's Bacon Factory at Elmswell; it has continued to flourish up to the present time.

But it is not so much with the development of pig-breeding and processing as an industry that we are concerned. The pig was an animal which was easy to rear and feed, and provided a regular supply of meat, not only to be eaten fresh, but very suitable for curing for later use. It could be kept not only on the farm, but behind the cottage, and for generations was a part of the rural economy. Moreover, feeding was helped by the fact that all manner of kitchen waste went into the swill-tub, where it was boiled up to make a fattening meal. To quote Tusser:

> '*Take pain with thy swill.*
> *Though heating be costly, such swill yet in store*
> *shall profit thy porklings a hundred times more.*'

Tusser reminds us that other natural products were gathered for pig-food. Of the poachers he says:

> '*Some prowleth for acorns, to fet up their swine*';

and

> '*October's good blast*
> *To blow the hog mast*'.

The killing of the cottager's pig was almost a ritual occasion, and friends and relations would gather round to witness the gory spectacle, and especially the later cutting up, perhaps in the hope of a share in the spoils. There is an old saying,

> *'Unless your bacon you would mar*
> *Kill not your pig without the "R".'*

As with oysters, there should be an R in the month, but for the good reason that the flesh keeps better in cold weather. Allan Jobson (1953) quotes an old proverb of 1664, 'Kill swine in or near the full of the Moon and the flesh will prove the better in boiling'. A waxing moon was always more propitious; as the moon waned, the flesh of the slain animal might shrink.

VETERINARY CARE

In *White's Directory of Suffolk* for 1844, Samuel Scott Baker is described as a Veterinary Surgeon and Shoeing Smith, and, as noted elsewhere, the farrier did include the care and treatment of horses, in sickness as well as in health, amongst the services he gave. The earliest forms of the instruments he used were made by the farrier himself, although in time more sophisticated versions were turned out commercially.

Horse-gags, farrier's gags or balling-irons took many forms, and were of different sizes for cart horse, light horse and pony. The common type in Suffolk was the U-shaped form with central ring; with this the mouth was forced open and the 'ball' (oddly-named as it is elongate and not spherical) administered by passing the hand through the ring, often almost up to the elbow. The ball-gun, of wood or iron, could be used to shoot the pellet down the throat, or a liquid dose or powder could be given with the drenching-horn, an adapted cow's horn. A popular story is told of a Suffolk horseman who called his small son to help when giving the horse a powder. 'I'll hold his mouth open, and you tip the powder down, and to make sure it goes down, I'll blow'. The horse blew first!

Rough teeth were filed down with a hefty rasp; for extraction, a lever with hooked head hinged at right angles was placed over the tooth, which was drawn

Fig. 16. VETERINARY INSTRUMENTS
1. 'Strike' firing-iron. 2. 'Pin' firing-iron. 3, 4, 5, 6. Horse-gags, farrier's gags, balling-irons; No. 5 is leather-covered. 7. Trocar and cannula. 8. Drenching-horn. 9. 'Wolf-tooth' chisel. 10. Ball-gun. 11. Tooth-rasp. 12, 13. Firing-irons; No. 12 is for cauterizing after docking. 14. Choking-rope, probang. 15. Cow-gag, for use with the probang. 16, 17, 20. Castrating clamps. 18. Fleam. 19. Fleam mallet.
(No. 14, $\frac{1}{12}$; remainder, $\frac{1}{6}$.)

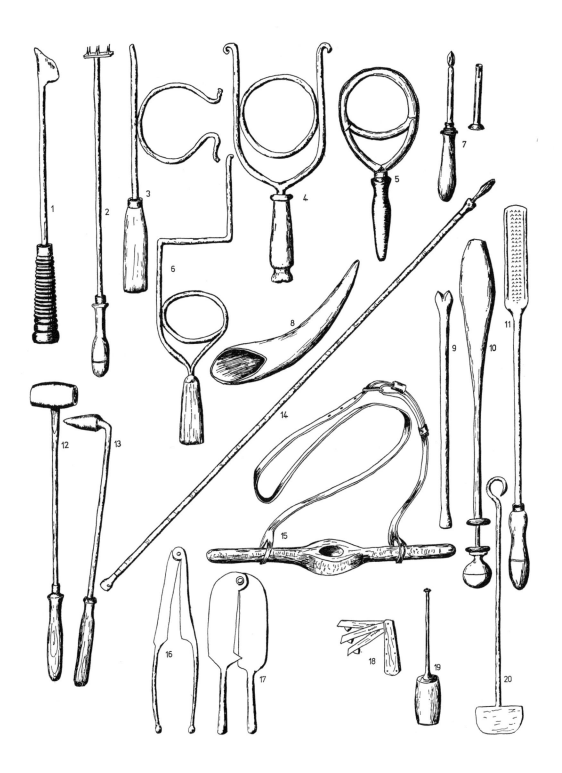

by a deft twist. Some farriers kept a smaller edition of this, with which they would perform the same service for a friend. A 'wolf-tooth', growing out into the cheek, was removed by using a chisel with grooved head. From William Freeman's diary:

'1854. March 1. Whayman taking Wolf's teeth from young horse.'

When swollen tendons gave trouble, a firing-iron with wedge-shaped blade, or with a flat head with spikes, was heated and applied. A firing-iron with a drum-shaped head was used to cauterize the stump after docking the tail.

It was not, of course, always necessary to call in the vet., or even the farrier; many of these instruments were kept on the farm for use as needed.

'1851. April 28. Fired the Grey Horse in the afternoon.'

Charles Freeman seems to have believed in wholesale treatment, for in 1827, on 10th February, he 'gave all my Horses a Ball each', and on the 13th 'Began to give all my Horses a powder each in some bran'.

Bleeding was resorted to frequently. The fleam used for this is a knife, usually with three blades each with a sharp tip set at right angles to the blade. It is applied to the vein and struck with a small mallet.

For the removal of an obstruction in the oesophagus of cattle a choking-rope (probang), a long tube of coiled wire, leather-covered, with a cane piston running its length inside, was pushed down the throat.

A remedy for the '*Foul*, the swelling of the hoofs in neat cattle' is given in *The Cattle Keeper's Guide* in the early nineteenth century, and seems to foreshadow the use of the seton needle. 'Take a hair rope, and draw it between the claws, till the swelling breaks and bleeds freely; and heal the wound with tar, turpentine and grease, mixed together'.

Another recipe from the same booklet is for

'A Wound by a Stab, or Thorn, where some parts of them are supposed to lodge in the Wound.

'Take black snails from commons, with as much black soap; which boil and mix into the consistency of a salve, and apply to the wound.'

That invariable stand-by, bleeding, is used

'To fasten Teeth in Sheep and Lambs.

'When you observe their teeth loose, which you will see by their not feeding, bleed them under the tail, and rub their gums with powder of mallow root.'

William Rogers's MS. booklet (Pl. 205), quoted in the notes on farriery, gives this recipe for 'blistering for a splint or spavin':

'Sublimate and spanish flies in fine powder each half a Drachm, tincture of euphorbium forty drops, oil of origanum an ounce and a half, nerve oil an ounce.'

8 Transport

(Pls 112–29)

It would be beyond the scope of this book to attempt a survey of all the various forms of transport used in the region in past times. Our aim is rather to recapture something of the atmosphere of an earlier age by recalling some specific occasions when journeys had to be undertaken, or tasks accomplished, and the means employed.

For the average countryman, his two feet had to suffice to carry him to and fro until the advent of the bicycle, but when it did arrive it opened up new fields to the enterprising owner. H. W. Damant, of Framlingham, told how his father toured 'from Land's End to John o' Groats' on a penny-farthing bicycle; this must have been in the 1890s.

Until the coming of the railways, long journeys were made by stage coach. When Charles Freeman went from Stowupland to London in 1822 for an eye operation, he travelled by 'Times Coach'. On 'a very wet morning' he 'Rode Bay Horse to Bury. Went to London by Times Coach outside'. It must have been an uncomfortable journey, for on his return he chose to ride inside and pay the extra fare. We have no record of the fare to Bury, but in 1819 the London to Colchester journey cost 16s. od. inside, 8s. od. outside. The Ipswich Blue Coach carried four inside and eleven outside, the Shannon Coach three inside and only one outside, charging £1. 1s. od. and 10s. od. respectively from Ipswich.* An advertisement in the *Suffolk Chronicle*, dated Saturday, 20th March 1824, reads:

THE ORIGINAL
IPSWICH COACH

Left the General Coach Office, Brook-street, Ipswich, every Morning at a Quarter before Nine o'clock, to the Golden Cross, Charing Cross, London; from whence it will return every Afternoon (Sundays excepted) at a Quarter past Twelve

* Copeland, 1968.

o'clock, leave the City at One o'clock precisely, and perform the journey to Ipswich with the greatest regularity, in Eight Hours and a Half.

WM. HORN
JAS. HAXELL & CO. } Proprietors.

This was not bad going, as stops were made for a change of horses every 10 miles or so, and the average speed was reckoned at 10 m.p.h.

For shorter journeys smaller vehicles were obtainable on hire. When Charles Freeman's widowed mother came to live with him in 1822, he drove her to her former home in Botesdale 'in a hired gig', and a few days later went to fetch her from that village in a post chaise, for which he paid £1. 0. 0 plus 2s. 6d. for the coachman and 9d. 'gate'. The gig was a light, high two-wheeler, without hood; the chaise was an enclosed carriage, the coachman riding one of the horses.

In 1856 William Freeman took a party from Stowupland to the Ipswich Ball; for this he hired a fly; the party included two ladies and three men. The term fly has been applied to a light two-seater carriage, but another definition refers to it as a hackney carriage.

The Tavener family of Ixworth Abbey used a landau, which could be opened or closed, and an elegant four-wheeled dog-cart with a folding step for the passenger. A basketwork shield placed over the wheel protected the lady's long skirts from being soiled as she stepped up. The original two-wheeled dog-cart had a rear compartment under the seat, with gridded sides for ventilation. The governess cart was in frequent use for shopping and, as its name implies, for the governess to take out her small charges for an airing. From the Henham Hall estate of the Earl of Stradbroke came a pony chaise, in which the lady of the house used to drive herself to church two generations ago.

A useful, and apparently local, conveyance was the ralli cart, used for general work around the estate, rather as the Land Rover is today, and by the game-keeper on the Henham estate.

The forerunner of the shooting brake was the game van; a magnificent specimen, formerly used by the Hon. Alastair Watson, first at Sudbourne and later at Chilles-ford, is now at the Abbot's Hall Museum. The interior is fitted with slotted bars from which the pheasants hung by the neck, and rounded rods to take the hares. When filled it must certainly have needed the two horses for which shafts are fitted.

Other road vehicles were designed for special functions—baker's van, butcher's cart, market cart for the itinerant tradesman, the horse-slaughterer's cart with windlass to hoist up the body for removal.

With the coming of the railways, the need for public road transport was lessened, but progress was slow. The line had reached Colchester by 1823, and it is of interest to note that efforts to hasten its progress farther north were led by that same John Chevallier who found time from his duties as rector and doctor to contribute to the improvement of agriculture and to champion any good cause. He took the chair at meetings at Ipswich as early as 1825, but the railway did not penetrate into Suffolk until 1847. So for many years the coaches still had to ply, at least to the nearest railway station.

Agriculture had its own special requirements for transport; it was probably in East Anglia that the four-wheeled wagon first came to be used as the main farm vehicle.

The most distinctive feature of the Suffolk wagon is the construction of the bed; the pole carries two braces branching off about midway between front and rear axles forming a Y-shaped frame. The form of the sides shows a wide variety, both in Suffolk and Essex, with open raves or solid side-boards. The floor is almost invariably cross-boarded, the boards running transversely; this gave greater strength than long-boarding, which was not necessary as the load was lifted clear and not run out as in the tumbril.

The harvest wagon had to run over the rough, uneven ground of the field; it was therefore advantageous to equip it with large wheels both fore and aft. This implied devising a means of allowing the wheel to turn, without making the body so high as to make loading difficult. So a waist was cut in the side to allow the wheel to turn, though to a limited extent. The dish of the wheel reduced the danger of side-rock, and gave more space for the load. The horses were led, either by the bridle or using a long rein, the carter walking alongside. Ladders fixed fore and aft increased the capacity.

The road wagon, on the other hand, needed the ability to negotiate street corners and was fitted with front wheels small enough to pass underneath the body; a seat for the driver hooked on to the front-board.

A wagon built by William Arbon of Mendlesham Green for John Brundish, of Tan Office Farm, near Mendlesham, and delivered on 22nd August 1839, cost £17. 0. 0, but in 1826 Charles Freeman paid Mr Green, Wheelwright, £22. 18. 0 for a new buck (body) for a wagon only.

The other general farm vehicle was the tumbril, a two-wheeled cart used for harvesting roots, spreading manure and even, when fitted with ladders, as an auxiliary aid in the harvest field. Its most notable feature was its tipping mechanism, which allowed swift and easy unloading. In the earlier type the body is secured to the bed by a wooden bar, the toe-stick, passing through hoops on the shafts.

When withdrawn it allows the body to be tilted, the movement being controlled by a hand-grip projecting from the top of the body. Two examples made at the Maldon Iron Works were first used at Rainham in Essex and later at Edwardstone in Suffolk. Later a wooden lever, pivoted at the centre, and turning into two iron brackets, simplified the process of tipping. The next stage was the replacement of the wooden lever by one of iron, and finally a vertical iron bar with peg-holes allowed tipping to be fixed at any angle.

When tar-macadam road surfaces made for smoother progress, some tumbrils were converted by fitting an iron undercarriage and wheels with pneumatic tyres.

Tumbrils were usually long-boarded to allow the load to run off easily, but in later years, when the traditional elm planks gave place to deal, the smoother surface obtainable made the stronger and less costly cross-boarding feasible.

A solution to the problem of cost involved in having both wagon and tumbril was provided by the hermaphrodite wagon, known locally as morphey, morphadite, hamphrodite, or almost any conceivable variation. It is in essence a tumbril with removable shafts; when wanted for harvest, a fore-carriage can be bolted on, with an extra pair of wheels, ladders placed in position, and lo! a harvest wagon is born. It is more usual in north Suffolk and Norfolk, though known as far north as south Yorkshire, and enjoyed great popularity. W. E. Wigg and Sons, of Barnby in north Suffolk, made one for Albert Tills of Kirby Cane, just over the Norfolk border. He sent it for repair to G. R. Briggs of Ellingham, and it was returned bearing the latter's name-plate as 'Maker'. When Miss Tills married Mr Hinsley of Flixton in Suffolk, it returned to the county of its origin.

The timber-jim or timber-drag shows the Y-shaped pole to advantage. One formerly used by H. W. Baldry, wheelwright, of Horham, has straked wheels. A larger vehicle from the Redgrave estate has hooped tyres.

Specially designed carts took bullocks to market; horse-boxes were, and still are, constructed to limit space and so avoid bruising. A moving spectacle, now more usual at agricultural shows than on the road, is that of the brewer's dray drawn by a team of Suffolks or Shires.

9 In and around the Home

In these days the production of equipment and objects of everyday use is calculated on the basis of increasing turnover and profits. Things are not intended to last, but designed to catch the public eye and increase sales. The work of the craftsman was inspired by his innate artistry, and his sense of satisfaction in turning out sound work. The results have endured, as the contents of our antique shops bear witness.

Interest in the past has an unaccountable fascination. The town-dweller who buys up a rural cottage 'suitable for modernization' discovers this when he begins to pull it about. The Victorian fireplace, when removed, reveals the great open hearth built in the sixteenth century; perhaps the fan which turned the roasting-spit is still in the chimney. It was made to revolve by the draught from the roaring fire, and in the basket of the spit could be roasted a whole lamb, or a massive joint of beef. At one time such a spit was powered by a dog, working a treadmill in a cage suspended on the wall. Even the cottage had its smoke-jack, which held the dangle-spit; one of these was found a few years ago in the chimney of a cottage at Eye, in Suffolk.

Across the fireplace would be a bar for the suspension of pothooks, or the kettle-tilter or 'idle-jack', or these might hang from the chimney-crane which swung out from the wall. Another common device was the bottle-jack, a brass cylinder operated by clockwork; this turned the suspended joint to and fro in front of the fire, and was often used in conjunction with the hastener, a curved screen which reflected the heat back on to the joint.

In the brick oven, a domed chamber built into the wall of the kitchen, a fire of faggots (often of hedge-cuttings or, in the heathland areas, furze) was laid.

Fig. 17. IN THE KITCHEN
1. Larding-needles. 2. Sugar-nippers. 3. Kettle-tilter, idle-jack. 4. Oven peel. 5. Pot-hook. 6. Dangle spit. 7. Ale-muller. 8. Nutmeg-grater. 9. Salamander. 10. Oven fork. 11. Chimney-crane, hake, gantry. 12. Pig-scraper and nail-remover (made from a cow's hoof). 13. Oxtail-skinner. 14. Roasting-spit.
(No. 2, $\frac{1}{5}$; 4, 5, 9, 10, 11 and 14, $\frac{1}{12}$; remainder, $\frac{1}{8}$.)

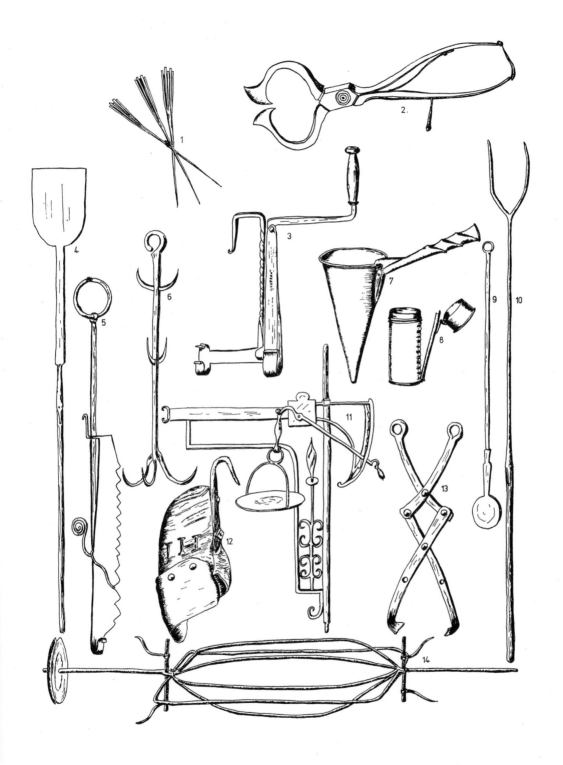

When the temperature was right, and the rear of the oven was white and soot-free, the embers were moved aside with the oven fork, or removed with the peel, which was used to place the bread and cakes in the oven. Cakes, pies and tarts were pushed to the back, meat-pies and sausage-rolls followed, then the milk-pudding, and last of all the bread. The hot ashes removed from the oven were taken over to the hearth, and used to heat a cauldron of water suspended on a hook, in readiness for the subsequent washing-up.

The pig has always formed a staple item in the diet of the countryman, and many a cottager would keep one or more in a sty at the end of the garden. The flesh was ideally suited for pickling, and formed a source of supply which would often last throughout the year. After the killing, the carcase was placed on the pig-bench, and the backbone or chine cut out. The body was singed, to rid it of as much hair as possible, and a pig-scraper used to remove the rest; the nails were extracted with a hook; a specimen in the Abbot's Hall Museum, made from the half of the cloven hoof of an ox, combines scraper and nail-extractor. The carcase was hung until wanted for cutting up, and kept open to the air by a pair of pig-stretchers or buckers.

Virtually nothing was wasted; various cuts of pork, bacon, ham and a fry using heart, liver, etc., were produced. Sausages were enclosed in natural skins derived from the intestines. Oddments went to the making of brawns, and the blood formed the main ingredient of black-puddings.

For the curing of hams a special ham-pot was used, of glazed earthenware, with deep upright sides and a kidney-shaped outline. Miss Ivy Cobbold, who farms at Stowupland, gave a recipe used by her mother for pickling. The ham was first well rubbed with common salt, and then placed in the pot with a mixture of salt, salt-petre, salt-prunel, dark brown sugar and treacle. It was turned daily, and the mixture ladled over it. When thoroughly pickled it was drained, and after a baking had taken place in the wall oven, the ham was placed therein to dry; then, sewn in muslin, it would hang from one of the ceiling hooks in the kitchen until wanted for the table. In course of time, a pickling preparation was made up by the whole-sale grocers, and sold in the village shop.

Fig. 18. IN THE DAIRY
1, 3. Butter-stamps, butter-prints. 2. Carrying-yoke. 4. Cheese-press. 5. Cream-fleeter. 6. Butter-scoop. 7. Butter-hand (one of a pair). 8. Keeler, made in 1892. 9. Barrel-churn (used with 8). 10. Pestle (for squeezing out the buttermilk, under water, in the keeler). 11. Table-churn (c.1850). 12. Milking-stool. 13. Milking-pail.
(Nos. 1, 3, 5, 6, 7 and 10, $\frac{1}{6}$; remainder, $\frac{1}{12}$.)

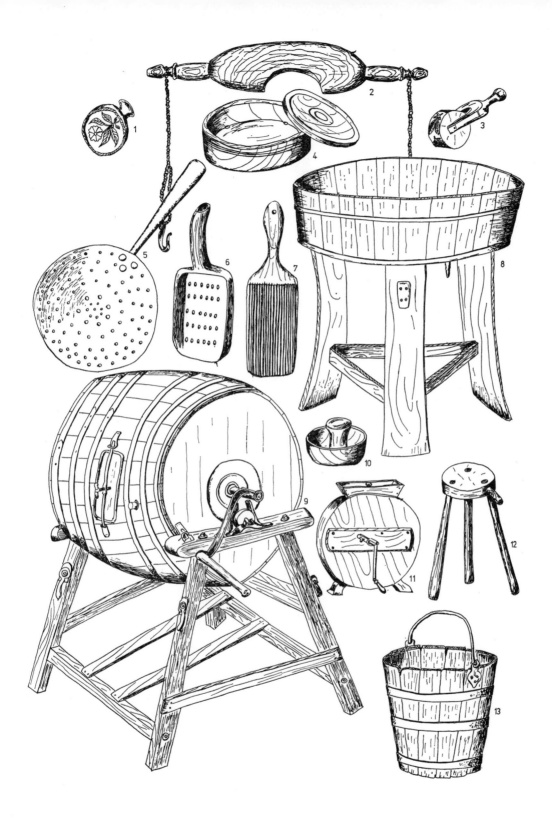

Miss Cobbold's farmhouse had not a suitable chimney, otherwise it was quite usual to hang the ham there, as Bloomfield relates in 'The Farmer's Boy':

> *'The well-wrought chimney rear its lofty head;*
> *Where since hath many a savoury ham been stor'd.'*

In the servants' hall at Christchurch Mansion, Ipswich, is a settle, the back of which opens to reveal a bacon-cupboard. Here the butler could sit and smoke a quiet pipe, the odour of home-cured bacon mingling with that of his shag.

Every farmhouse had its dairy, with all the gear necessary for making butter and cheese, and in many a cottage could be found a table-churn or paddle-churn; in later times came the 'atmospheric' churn, a tall glass bottle similar to those to be seen in the confectioner's, with a screw-top lid from which depended wooden paddles turned by a handle protruding from the lid.

Milk was left overnight in a wide, low bowl of earthenware or tinned iron to allow the cream to rise. This was skimmed off using a fleeter, a circular, shallow, perforated scoop of brass, copper or tin, with a short handle. When enough cream had been saved, it was poured into the wooden churn. The earlier models were either barrel-shaped or of sub-triangular section, turning horizontally; in later types the barrel was fitted to turn end-over-end. It seems likely that the triangular churn was in the nature of an attempt to speed up the process by causing the contents to 'flop' rather than roll; this was even more effectively achieved in the end-over-end churn. Bloomfield well knew the sound of the butter as it flopped within the churn:

> *'Slow rolls the churn, its load of clogging cream*
> *At once foregoes its quality and name:*
> *From knotty particles first floating wide*
> *Congealing butter's dashed from side to side.'*

When Mrs Cobbold married in 1892, a keeler was made for her by the cooper. It is a shallow tub on legs, and in it the butter was washed as it came out of the churn. The washing was done by hand, but in hot summer weather the process was helped by using a kind of pestle, rather like a darner with deeply turned edges. It was made of willow, and with it the buttermilk was expressed from the butter. At that time Mrs Cobbold had a barrel-churn. Round about 1910 she changed to an end-over-end churn, in which the butter is washed by repeated pails of water. It is then drained and removed by means of a perforated willow scoop to a butter-worker, a shallow wooden trough on legs, with a roller with parallel blades. This squeezes out any remaining water, and the butter is beaten into pounds and half-pounds with butter-hands. Stamps or moulds are used to decorate the finished product; they may be circular, or take the form of rollers impressing a continuous pattern.

William Camden (*Britannia*, ed. 1607) was eulogistic indeed on the subject of Suffolk butter:

'For quantity and quality this county doth excel, and vendeth it at London and elsewhere. The child not yet come to and the old man who is past the use of teeth, eateth no softer, the poor man no cheaper (in this shire), the rich no wholesomer food, I mean in the morning. It was half of our Saviour's bill of fare in his infancy: "Butter and honey shall he eat".'

But if Suffolk is extolled for its butter, it is execrated for its cheese. Not however by Camden, who has this to say:

'*Cheese*—Most excellent are made therein, whereof the finest are very thin, as intended not for food but digestion. I remember when living in Cambridge the cheese of this county was preferred as the best. If any say that Scholars' palates are incompetent judges, whose appetites make coarse diet seem delicate unto them, let them know that Pantaleon the learned Dutch physician counted them equal at least with them of Parma in Italy.'

Camden's assessment did not find the concurrence of many. Raynbird is not sparing of words on the subject:

'*Bang*—Suffolk cheese, made of milk several times skimmed, therefore very hard and tough, otherwise called Suffolk thump. . . . the only merit allowed it is that of keeping well, and consequently being the best for ships' stores. As Suffolk folk get the benefit in the butter they are quite ready to join in the laugh against this product of their "three-times skimmed sky-blue" . . . a story is told, that a parcel of Suffolk cheese being packed up in an iron chest and put on board a ship bound to the West Indies, the rats, allured by the scent, gnawed a hole in the chest, but could not penetrate the cheese. . . . The following *elegant* couplets are very current in the county:

> "*Those who made me were uncivil*
> *For they made me harder than the devil;*
> *Knives won't cut me, fire won't sweat me,*
> *Dogs bark at me, but can't eat me*".'

Cheese is made by the addition of rennet to the milk. A recipe for the preparation of rennet from 'a calf's bag, maw or stomach' is given in Marshall's *Rural Economy of Norfolk*. After salting, it should be kept for twelve months. Then 'take a handful of the leaves of sweet-briar, the same quantity of the leaves of the dog rose, and the like quantity of bramble leaves'. These are boiled, with added salt, then poured over the maw; the final touch is the addition of 'a good sound lemon, stuck round with about a quarter of an ounce of cloves'. By the turn of the century, rennet could be bought, ready for use. William Rogers of Ilketshall bought one shilling's worth from the dairy in Beccles in June 1908. Cottage cheeses were made in shallow wooden presses, perforated to allow the whey to escape; a farmhouse kitchen might be equipped with a heavy iron press; one was recently seen in East Suffolk.

In 1903 William Rogers paid 4s. od. to his father for malting two coombs of barley, but from 1904 onwards his account book shows regular expenditure twice a year, usually in the autumn and early summer, on 1 bushel of malt and 1 lb. of hops, for which he paid 6s. od. This would make about twenty gallons of beer, in readiness for harvest, and for Christmas. In the autumn, too, he purchased his brewing licence, for 4s. od.

Sometimes brewing would begin during the afternoon of the day previous to the big day, with the malt left overnight in the brewing tub or mash tub to ensure thorough steeping. The following morning an early start was made, as the copper had to be brought to the boil. The malt was thoroughly mixed by hand and then transferred to the keeler which, like the butter keeler, was raised on legs. A wooden tap at the base projected into the inside of the keeler, where the wilsh, a sheath of wickerwork, was fitted over it to prevent the escape of the grains. The malt was then covered with water, and a third pail of boiling water from the copper was ladled into it with the wooden hand-cup. This was cut from a single piece of wood, generally willow, and sometimes had a grooved handle from which the liquid could be poured for testing. Next the keeler was covered with the rack, often a natural forked branch, covered with a cloth, and left to steep. Some ten gallons of boiling water were then added, and the mixture thoroughly stirred with the masher.

Meantime the mash-tub had been so placed that the the liquid could be run off into it from the keeler, after allowing it to stand for four hours. This gave the first 'wort'. Further water was added to the malt in the keeler to form the second wort. If it was intended to keep this separate as 'small beer', the first wort was poured into the copper, where three quarters of the hops would be added, and the whole boiled for four hours, after which it was drained through a sieve into the mash-tub. The second wort would then be boiled in the copper, with the remaining hops. Often the two were combined to form a single brew. When the mixture had cooled down, a pint of yeast was added to cause fermentation. The yeast could be used over and over again, and was passed from house to house.

The beer was stored in casks, which stood when ready for use on the beer-stool, with a stepped tilter to angle the cask as needed. Pouring into the cask brought into play the funnel, known in Suffolk as the 'tunnel'.

An interesting item in William Rogers's accounts occurs whenever he visits the town for supplies, 'X Keys 9*d*'. He evidently sampled the publican's brew as a change from his own, leaving his horse and trap in charge of the 'oystler'.

Hops were grown extensively in Suffolk,* especially in the area round Stowmarket, where an annual Hop Fair was held in September.†

It has been said by a connoisseur of wine that it can be made only from the grape; country folk will have none of this. There is at the present time what amounts to a craze for home wine-making, from prepared packs, but the rural housewife has always made wine from a great variety of wild plants. In July 1822 Charles Freeman wrote in his diary: 'Made Wine with Gooseberries and Red and White Currants.—Memorandum. Juice $26\frac{1}{4}$ Pints. Water 56 Pints. 2 Sts. 8 lb. sugar put to Wine. $10\frac{1}{4}$ Gall. before putting in Sugar. Sugar increased it 2 Gall.'

It will soon be an experience beyond living memory for the regular household requirements, other possibly than milk, to be delivered at the door. The butcher used to drive up perched high on a seat placed above the body of his cart, to save all possible space for his stock of meat. The milkman rattled up with his trolley, or a horse-drawn float, poured milk from the churn into a hand-can, and served it with a pint or half-pint ladle, bearing the stamp of the Inspector of Weights and Measures. The baker, too, made his rounds in a van, or with a hand-cart. The butcher's boy delivered your joint of beef or mutton borne on a shallow tray carried on his shoulder.

Sugar reached the grocer in the form of sugar-loaves, conical in form, and standing up to 4 ft 6 ins high. These he would break up into quite sizeable lumps, which had to be further reduced at home with the sugar-nippers.

Table knives were of good steel, not of the stainless variety; they were cleaned in a rotary machine with slots to take the blades, one especially large for the carver.

The housewife of today can have little conception of the effort which went into the washday of her grandmother's time. Not only was the actual washing done manually, but there were no handy packets of powder guaranteed to wash whiter than white, or softer than soft. The ashes from the wood fire in wall-oven or

* Trist, 1971, quoting R. E. Prothero, *English Farming Past and Present* (1917), and Thomas Tusser.
† Charles Freeman's diary, 1828.

kitchen range were placed in a leech or letch, a wooden tub holding about a gallon of water, and having a perforated base. Water was poured on the ashes, and strained through muslin into a large tub, perhaps the 'bucking tubbe' referred to in a document of 1572 listing expenses at Hengrave Hall in West Suffolk.

Washing techniques ranged from the scrubbing-board used over the kitchen sink, to the dolly-tub with legged dolly-stick, and machines of much earlier vintage than is usually supposed. These were spring-loaded wringers, in combination with a rotating box. In the earliest type, the pressure was supplied by a system of weights suspended on bars, with separate wheels to turn box and wringer, but an improved model was fitted with an arrangement of cogs sliding on a spindle, to engage either the wringer or box as required; the pressure was controlled by a screw. Yet another type used locally was operated by a lever which, when pushed backwards and forwards, activated a kind of miniature dolly-stick.

A machine which, despite the considerable effort involved in its use, continued in popularity over a very long period, was the box-mangle, almost indispensable in the larger farmhouses, and often found in even cottage homes, where washing was 'taken in'. A large chest, weighted by its contents which in East Anglia consisted of a load of flints (large blocks in areas where quarried stone was available), was propelled to and fro on wooden rollers by a crank, the motion controlled by chains attached to either end and to the crank, so that the direction was automatically reversed at the end of the track. It was used mainly for the pressing of such large articles as sheets. These were first wrung out by hand, then wrapped round the rollers. When the process was complete a lever was lowered, so that the box ran up it, lifting sufficiently to allow the rollers to be removed.

Sheets and garments were often laid out on the grass for bleaching, but the blue-bag was used for the last rinse to ensure whiteness; blueing powder has been in use since the seventeenth century. Clothes pegs, often cut out of a single piece of ash or other suitable wood, were made and sold by gypsies. Starch could be prepared at home from potatoes, grated and soaked in cold water.

Fig. 19. LIGHTING, BREWING AND GENERAL
1. Candle-snuffers. 2. 'Economy' candlestick. 3. Lanthorn. 4. Candlestick with wind-shield. 5. Candle-holder. 6. Lamp-wick trimmer. 7. 'Lazy-tongs'. 8. Brewing masher. 9. Faucet with wilsh (brewing). 10. Brewing-funnel ('tunnel' in Suffolk). 11. Dipper for sampling the brew (made from a single block of wood). 12. Corn-scuppit. 13. Butcher's tray. 14. 'Cat' (used as a work-basket stand; an iron form was a plate-warmer). 15. Glove-powdering flask. 16. Bowl used in 3-pin bowling. 17. Marking-out frame for 3-pin bowling.
(Nos. 1, 6 and 15, $\frac{1}{3}$; 8, 12, 13 and 17, $\frac{1}{12}$; remainder, $\frac{1}{6}$.)

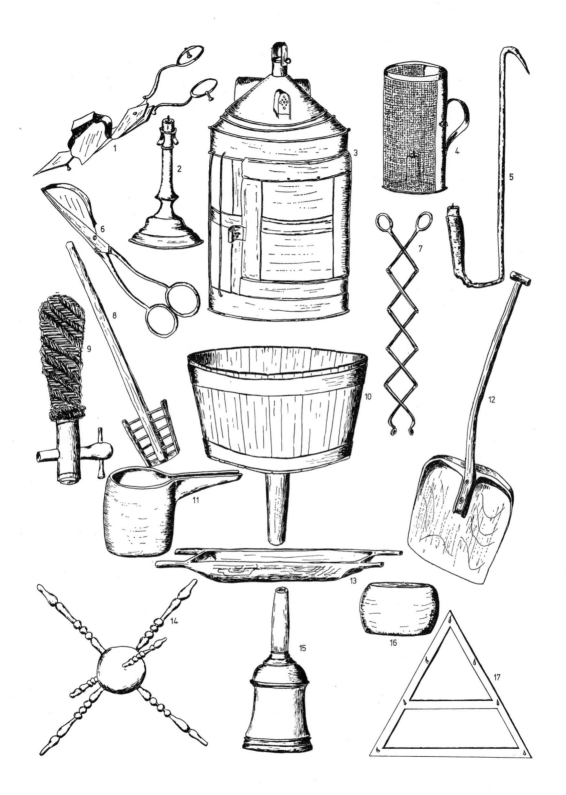

The flat-iron or sad iron was used, but seems to have enjoyed less popularity here than elsewhere, e.g. in the north of England. The box-iron seems to have found most favour, to judge from the number which have survived, although they were not cheap, relatively speaking. In 1873, William Clouting made two new heaters for a box-iron at a charge of 3s. 4d. The 'box' had a rear plate which could be raised to remove and replace the heater, which was heated in the fire. The charcoal iron was provided with a funnel to generate the draught essential to keep the charcoal aglow. Even a petrol iron was produced, with a cylindrical fuel tank.

The earliest goffering iron, for making pleats, took the form of a slender pair of tongs, with blades of round section. The Italian iron consisted of a poker-like rod which was heated in the fire and then inserted into a sheath which was supported on a stand; the pleat was formed by pressing the garment over this, or the material could be smoothed by drawing it over the iron from side to side. For finer crimping there was the goffering or crimping machine, resembling a miniature wringer, with iron rollers grooved along their length. Heaters were inserted into the rollers, which were turned as the cloth passed between them.

Sheets were smoothed with the slickenstone, a wooden or glass utensil resembling a stocking darner in form. The airing of clothes was often carried out by placing them in the wall-oven, or Dutch oven, after baking was finished.

In country districts where gas, even after its introduction in the towns, was not available, candles and lamps and the rushlight were in use. The rushlight was made by repeated dipping of the rush in tallow, allowing each layer to set before the process was repeated. It was held in a holder hinged to allow the rush to be inserted in the jaws, which were then closed by a counterweight. Candles were made in moulds, with wicks of knitted cotton. The wick needed repeated trimming to prevent smouldering, and for this purpose snuffers were used, some of the simple scissor type, others with a vertical knife, either with or without a spring action. Snuffers were often delicately fashioned, in silver, with a tray to hold them when not in use. Candlesticks had a shallow saucer to catch the drips, and an extinguisher of conical form, standing on a peg at the side. Economy, then as now, had to be taken into consideration, and a type of candlestick was obtainable with a hollow stem; when the candle had burnt down the stub was pushed out from below, and affixed to a spiked cap which could then be fitted over the top of the stem, thus giving the candle a new if brief lease of life.

The candle too was the source of illumination for the pendent candle-holder which was made to hook into the wall of the barn or stable (a somewhat risky procedure); in the search for museum material one of these holders of eighteenth-century pattern, holding the stump of a twentieth-century candle, was actually found in a farm outbuilding, hooked into the wall. The candle was also used in the carriage-lamp, in which a spring in the long stem kept it to burning level as it melted. A candle-holder with a gauze wind-shield could be used out of doors or, with a cover, by the housemaid when dusting under the bed.

The great storm lanthorn had windows made from the pared-down strips of cow's horn. Even the bullseye lantern, or dark lantern, which could be darkened by turning the inner core, and was used by the village constable in a form which hooked on to the belt, was candle-lit at first, though later by oil. Striking a light using flint, steel and tinder must have required skill and practice. The early sulphur-tipped match was ignited from the smouldering tinder, to give a flame to light the candle.

About the middle of the nineteenth century, or a little later, the introduction of paraffin brought in the lamp, with wick and glass chimney. Trimming of the wick was still necessary, as it had been for the candle, in order to give a steady flame; for this purpose wick-scissors, flat-bladed with a 'wall' to prevent the shreds from falling, were introduced. In the present century came the pressure lamp in which the spirit was volatilized and burnt through a mantle.

The forerunner of the modern electric blanket was the warming pan, of copper or brass, with a long handle with which it could be moved about the bed to warm evenly. It was filled with hot embers from the fire and, unlike its successor, when not in use it made an attractive wall-ornament. Hot-water bottles were of earthenware, and rather less likely to leak than their rubber counterparts, but a brick heated by the fire, and wrapped in a blanket, or even the oven shelf similarly guarded, served almost equally well. In these days it is possible to buy an electric boot-dryer; formerly a boot-shaped bottle filled with hot water helped to effect this.

10 Life, Work and Play

There can be no surer means of presenting a picture of daily life than to invoke the actual word, written or spoken, of those who live that life. It may be argued that this will reflect only the individual; this is not really so, for in recounting his own doings he must bring us into contact with those with whom he lives and works—and plays, and so give us at least his reactions to them.

The diaries of Charles and William Freeman are particularly rich sources of such records; it is not often that so full an account of daily doings is available. Father and son are relating their experiences over two periods separated by an interval of twenty years. There is continuity, but there is also change. At the age of twenty-three, Charles found himself farming in his own right, though evidently in constant consultation with his grandfather and uncles, one a doctor and one a parson (also farming). Living at first just over the Norfolk border, at Thorpe Abbotts, he was a frequent visitor to his aunt at Burgate, and inevitably saw much of his cousin, Mary Ann Freeman. In 1821, at the age of twenty-four, he moved to Stowupland Hall, and farmed a considerable acreage in that parish, and in the neighbouring Earl Stonham, and the Creetings. He still continued his visits to Burgate, although this meant a ride of nearly double that from Thorpe. So gradually he and his cousin came to the realization that they wanted a settled relationship. This was no case of love at first sight. On 16th March 1823, he wrote: 'Ann and I concluded when we were to M.'. But on 13th April, 'Mrs. F. did not like Ann to be M. at Stowmarket', and yet another month later, 'Ann and I finally agreed'.

A somewhat unusual custom seems to be indicated by the entry on Tuesday, 20th May: 'Cut up Wedding Cake in afternoon', for the wedding was on May 22nd. 'Showery day. Got up in morning $\frac{1}{2}$ past 4. Quite unwell. Married at Burgate at 9 O'clock. Mr. Cooke gave Ann away. Mrs. Cooke and John Freeman were there. Emma Freeman and Caroline Cooke were Bridesmaids. Dined at Bungay. Drank tea at Yarmouth.' (Dinner was usually at 2.0 p.m., tea at 5.0.)

The firm resolve of both father and son to leave out nothing worthy of record

113. *Two tumbrils made at the Maldon Iron Works, and used by the Gunary family first at Rainham, Essex, and later at Edwardstone, Suffolk. The tipping mechanism is the 'toestick', a wooden bar held in position by iron loops on the shafts.*

114. *Two tumbrils, one with iron pivoting lever, the other with graduated vertical iron bar, to regulate tipping.*

115. *Harvest wagon used by A. G. Saunders of Cranley Hall, Eye; straked wheels, probably formerly hooped, judging by the number of spokes.*

116. *Two-horse road-wagon; the driver's seat is hooked into two eyes on the front board.*

117. *A hermaphrodite wagon as it was discovered on Abbey Farm, Flixton.*

118. *A miller's wagon at Framlingham. The horses are wearing fly-nets.*

119. *A horse-drawn milk trolley, Holywell Dairy, Ipswich.*

120. *A carrier's cart. The carrier conveyed the occasional passenger as well as goods.*

121. *Delivery of goods by traction engine at Leiston.*

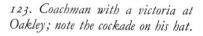

122. Game van used by the Hon. Alastair Watson at Sudbourne and Chillesford; built about 1912.

123. Coachman with a victoria at Oakley; note the cockade on his hat.

124. Horse-drawn gig in Stoke Street, Ipswich.

125. Pony chaise used by the grandparents of the present Earl of Stradbroke at Henham Hall.

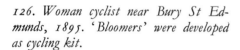

126. Woman cyclist near Bury St Edmunds, 1895. 'Bloomers' were developed as cycling kit.

127. The village postman, Helmingham, 1912.

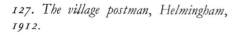

128. *Horse-drawn fire-engine of the Nayland Fire Brigade.*

129. *The Framlingham motor fire-engine and crew.*

130. *A day's outing by pleasure brake.*

131. The Great Eastern Railway's motor-bus, transporting passengers to and from Southwold, where there was no railway.

132. Beating the Bounds at Mendlesham, 5th April 1913.

133. A dairying class at Wickham Market, c. 1909. These classes were arranged jointly by the Suffolk and Norfolk County Councils.

134. *The staff of Stowupland Hall in the time of the Freeman family, c. 1860.*

135. *Robert Armstrong at the barrel organ in Shelland church.*

136. *John Hayward, butcher, Needham Market; he dressed thus weekdays and Sundays, tucking his apron under his coat when in church.*

137. *Lord Rendlesham's keepers and beaters at Eyke.*

leads inevitably on occasion to unconscious humour. '1830. March 9. Mrs. F. put to bed at half past nine at night of a fine Boy.—Got off all my Turnips.'

When in later years the 'fine boy' himself read these diaries, he left a pencilled note, 'These Books looked over, when *ill* by Wm. Freeman in Charlie's bedroom, with a fire, with Lumbago. Spring of 1915.' But his own entries have the same quality: '1850. April 27. The Revd. Smith dined with us. Roof of Backhouse fell in.'

A letter from Charles Freeman reads, 'C. R. Freeman desires his respectful Compliments to the Revd. R. W. Smith and gives him a general invitation to Dinner every Sunday directly after the forenoon Service either with or without a friend.

Stowupland Sept. 8th., 1845.'

This may have been in appreciation of the fact that when Charles became too deaf to follow the sermon, Mr. Smith obligingly loaned him the MS., and copies of a number of the sermons are amongst the Freeman papers. The clergy were highly esteemed, and were largely drawn from the ranks of the gentry and landed families. The Freemans took their religion seriously, and William in particular studied the Scriptures methodically every Sunday afternoon, as well as attending church often twice or more, often in the different villages where other members of the family were established.

Sickness, too, was not merely a hazard of existence, but attributable to an act of the Almighty.

'1827. October 18. Mr. Sheldrake went home about $\frac{1}{2}$ past one this morning and found his sister insensible. She expired about $\frac{1}{2}$ past three after being bled by Mr. Spencer Freeman. She went to bed the evening before at 11 o'clock in excellent spirits.

'October 19. The Coroner sat on Elizabeth Sheldrake and the Jury returned a Verdick. Died by the Visitation of God of a Fit of Apoplexy.'

Bleeding was regarded as a sovereign remedy for many ailments (though not efficacious in this case!), and when Charles was 'very Ill in bed with a burning pain in my knees and legs. Mr. Freeman came and bled me'.

When, in 1822, Charles Freeman developed eye trouble, it was decided that he should go to London to see a specialist. This he did, but after some days, dissatisfied with the slow progress and apparent lack of attention by the surgeon, he decided to take the matter into his own hands: 'Applyed Two Leeches to Eye. Received great Ease.'

Not only the surgeons believed in bleeding. On 18th February 1826, the 'Old Bay Mare fell down in tumbril and broke two of her ribs. Dr. Pizzey bled her'.

Vaccination was a comparatively recent discovery, or had not been sufficiently proved by 1828 to warrant its being made obligatory (this happened in 1853). On 23rd September 1828, Charles Freeman's cousin, Spencer Freeman, vaccinated his daughter Mary, then aged sixteen months. Presumably this had taken, for a week later, on 1st October to be precise, Charles wrote in his diary: 'Mr. Freeman vaccinated me from my little girl in four places, two on each arm'.

Charles Freeman seems to have been zealous in pursuit of the wrongdoer, and as a result we learn from his writings something of the way the law worked at that time.

'1824. April 22. Found Gun I lost in Water Meadow. Got Hand Bills printed offered 10£ Reward.

April 23. Sent James Lockwood to Gaol for stealing Gun.

26. Took James Warren to Mr. Matthews. Do. to Mr. Daltons. Do. to Stowmarket as an evidence against James Lockwood for felony.

30. Went to Ipswich Quarter Sessions to appear against James Lockwood for stealing gun. J.L. got 12 months imprisonment and to be privately whipped.

December 28. . . . found out I had a lamb taken out of fold and carryed away the skin was found Decr. 20th in River below Mr. Cross's Mill, Stowupland. Sent letter to Stow to have hand Bills printed offering 50£ Reward to convict stealers of Lamb'.

We do not hear the result of this publicity, but at the next Quarter Sessions at Bury St Edmunds on 17th January 1825 he reports how Wm. Rase and G. Southgate were sent to gaol to take their trial at the Assizes for stealing flour, etc. Either he does not record the result of that trial or George Southgate must have languished in prison for two years awaiting trial, for on 12th January 1827, at the Ipswich Quarter Sessions, he received a sentence of transportation for seven years for stealing flour.

On 10th February 1827 Charles Freeman sent Philip Daines, belonging to Ireland, to Ipswich Gaol as a vagrant.

Less than a fortnight later, on discovering that two pieces of apple wood were missing from the meadow in front of the house, he went to see a Mr Marriott, a Justice of the Peace, and applied for a search warrant, for which he paid half-a-crown. Armed with this, he went to the house of Thomas Race, where he found the wood, and sent Thomas to gaol to await trial. This took place before a magistrate at Creeting St Peter; the defendant was given a sentence of six months in the House of Correction.

The determination of the general public to stamp out crime is shown by the following advertisement which appeared in the Suffolk Chronicle for Saturday, 6th February 1824:

IPSWICH ASSOCIATION
For Prosecuting Felons and other Offenders

The Annual Meeting of the Subscribers to this Association will be held at the Golden Lion, in Ipswich, on Tuesday next, the 10th of February instant; when and where the Subscribers and other persons desirous of joining the said Association are requested to attend.

Ipswich, February 6th., 1824.   B. BRAME, Agent.
Dinner at Three o'clock.

Periodically, some local devotee of local history awakens to the realization that the ancient ceremony of 'Beating the Bounds' (Pl. 130) had fallen into disuse. Hence the following entry in Charles Freeman's diary:

'1830. May 18. Went the Bounds of Stowmarket and dined at Kings Head 20 sat down to Dinner. The bounds had not been gone before for 34 or 35 years. Dinner at King's Head 7.6. Hostler Men to spend, &c. 2.6.'

Both Charles Freeman and his son William went to the Great Exhibition of 1851 at the Crystal Palace, but William wisely decided to let his father go on his own, so that he himself could satisfy his wider interests, and do the rounds of the city. On 20th June he went to the Exhibition and stayed until 7 p.m., dined in the Strand, took a bus to Cremorne, returned to Blackfriars Bridge by steamer and 'saw her Majesty and the Prince in the Park'. On the following day he made calls in the morning, went to the Exhibition at 12 noon, and to the Chinese Junk in the evening. Sunday—to the Roman Catholic Chapel in St George's Fields to witness High Mass 'performed by Cardinal Wiseman', and during the following week to the Surrey Gardens 'to hear some singing', to Kensale Green Cemetery, the Monument, Custom House, Coal Exchange, the docks, the Zoo, a review in Regent's Park, with the band playing, the Polytechnic ('not now worth seeing'), the National Gallery, Madame Tussauds, the Argyle Rooms and 'Wyed's Globe', ending up with an evening at Bailey's Hippodrome. Home by train on Sunday, and to church in the afternoon.

Although in those days it was not possible to conjure up a learned discourse at the turn of a switch, or take a course of lessons in a foreign tongue with the aid of a record-player, or register for a session of University Extension Lectures, occasions for enlightment or aesthetic satisfaction there were in plenty. December 1851 saw William Freeman attending a French lesson at the reading-room at Stowmarket, a concert on the following evening, and the next day dining with Mr Spencer Freeman to meet MacDougall and Burman 'the Arctic voyageurs, and found them jolly fellows'. A week later he 'had a party of 30 to a Quadrille party, retired to rest at 4½ past next morning'. At the New Year he entertained to dinner '21 Cousins and other friends included. A Mr. Beau from Epping, dined and stayed with us and we found him a pleasant and Gentlemanly man'.

Other occasions included a lecture on Chemistry at Stowmarket by Mr Geo. Downes, the schoolmaster, Mons. Jullien's concert at Ipswich, a visit to the 'Florentine Model', 'a very extraordinary piece of mechanism', and what must have been a memorable occasion in 1856 when a party of ten went to Norwich 'to hear Madame Goldschmidt Lind and were greatly entertained', and no wonder, for this was of course Jenny Lind, 'the Swedish Nightingale', one of the most notable sopranos of all time. She would then be thirty-six, and at the height of her career as a concert singer, having devoted herself to this when she gave up opera in 1849. She was married to her accompanist, Otto Goldschmidt.

Perhaps a lecture on 'The Social Influence of Women', by a Mrs Balfour, held in Stowmarket on 11th April 1851, was a foreshadowing of Christabel Pankhurst's 'Women's Social and Political Union', founded in 1903, which won the right of suffrage for women, and eventually their entry into Parliament, with all its consequences.

For those in the same walk of life as the Freemans, the social round helped to relieve the cares of business; they rode and drove round the countryside to tea and dinner, and even to breakfast, with friends and relatives. Family ties were strong; the era of 'inability to communicate' between parents and offspring had not arrived. This was equally so amongst the labouring classes, with less leisure and fewer means of getting about.

Mrs Felgate of Playford recalled how, in the early days of her married life, about 1908, she and her husband would walk from Playford to Kirton, a distance of about ten miles, to see his brother. At that stage they had one child who would be pushed the whole way in the pram—and of course all the way back again in the evening. A few years later found them cycling to Grundisburgh, some three or four miles away, each with a child clinging to the back. When the third child arrived, her husband made her a box-carrier, but she soon gave up the attempt— 'I was too narvous, y'see!' Her father, George Pinner, had lived in Grundisburgh all his life, and had never been to any towns other than Ipswich and

Woodbridge, respectively seven and three miles distant. He had never seen the sea, and until at the time of his wife's last illness they went to live with his daughter, he had never seen a train. One day the Rector of Burgh, the next village to Grundisburgh, saw him clipping a hedge. Mrs Felgate tells the story of this encounter:

' "George", 'e say, "they tell me you've never seen the sea." "That's roight", 'e say. "Well", 'e say, "look 'ere! If you like to go to Felixstowe one day, I'll pay for your food and drink, what you 'ev, and pay you a day's wages. That won't corst you nawthing." But 'e wouldn't go.'

So George Pinner died without ever having seen the sea, although this was not the only attempt to get him there.

'The people that live next door; they'd got a son i' the army. He came home on leave. He came in here the Friday night. He say, "Pop", he say, "I'm goin' to have a horse and waggonette from Grundisburgh termorrer", 'e say, "and go to Felixstowe—take my younger brothers and sisters", 'e say, "and I want you to come with me." "Oh!", 'e say, "I don't know." 'E say, "Do *you* come", 'e say, "that won't corst y'anything." "I'll let you know in the mornin' ", 'e say. So after Bill was gone indoors the first thing 'e say to me, "I ain't goin' y'know,—suthen moight haapen." '

Mrs Felgate still used to visit her daughter in Witnesham when she was in her eighties, and at the best of times it was something of an undertaking. She had about an hour's walk to get the bus into Ipswich, where she got another bus to Witnesham, about another five or six miles. On one occasion she got the wrong bus out of Ipswich, and although the conductor was most obliging in setting her down at the most convenient point, she had an extra two-mile walk. 'I got there all right,' she said.

William Freeman's visits to relatives—he seems to have had cousins in almost every village within a twelve-mile radius of his home—brought him into frequent contact with his cousin Charlotte at Debenham, and for a time his diary was filled with his eulogies of this pretty, amiable, fascinating, graceful and justly admired creature. He was never happier than when riding or driving with her round the countryside, picking flowers for her, or accompanying her to hear 'Mr. Bowles' Concert of the Creation'. On at least two occasions he was so overcome by his feelings that he wrote: 'Ah! if only she were not my cousin',—and yet his father and mother were first cousins.

Lotty, as he called her, made one of the party that he drove to Stowmarket on 30th December 1851, 'to witness the ceremony of Miss Emily Hollingsworth's wedding. The church was crowded and I had a good view of the ceremony at the altar by standing on the window cill in the chancel, there were 8 bridesmaids, and with the exception of their driving through the town, it was an imposing and gratifying scene.' Another member of the party was Joyce Ridley, whom he was later to marry, and one cannot help wondering what were her thoughts when in due course she saw this entry.

Education was then, as now, conditioned by the financial standing of the parents. In 1828 Thomas Ridley, Brandy Merchant, of Ipswich, took his daughter Ellen to France to complete her schooling. He was accompanied by his son, George, and George's friend, Charles Freeman, who has given a graphic account of their excursion. They spent the night of the 31st July in London, and the next morning 'went and saw the Thames Tunnell before breakfast. got our Passports and went to Brighton at night. myself, Mr. G. Ridley, Mr. Thos. Ridley and Miss Ellen Ridley.'

'August 2. Saw Brighton. Went on board Steam Packet at 2 o'clock in Afternoon and landed at Dieppe in France about ½ past 2 on the Sunday morning being very Ill with sea sickness in coming over.

'August 3. Staid at Dieppe all day. it has a very stony beach. there is a crucifix on the quay. the head dress of the lower and middle class of females appear very singular and has remained unchanged for time immemorial.

'August 4. Left Miss Ridley at school at Dieppe at Miss Moncer's. departed for Rouen at 10 by Diligence drawn by 6 Horses. Postilion riding on near Wheel Horse and driving 5 others. arrived at Rouen at 5. dined at table d'hôte Hotel de Normandie.'

In 1847 Ellen Ridley's niece, Alice, was sent to school at the Institution de Madame Dumay, Rue de Vaugirard, Paris. The fees were 325 francs a term, but by the time extras for music, Italian, books, hot baths and other luxuries were added the bill came to anything from 600 to nearly 1,000 francs. In addition there was a monthly account for board of fifteen or twenty pounds sterling. The franc at that time stood at 25 to the pound.

William Freeman was sent to Mr Downes' Academy at Wickham Market. On 17th March 1841 his father wrote to him urging him to write to his sister Mary. She received sixpence every time she wrote to William at school and he would be given the same. Referring to his eleventh birthday, his father says that now he is a year older he must try to be a year wiser and do all that his tutor Mr Downes tells him.

As is not infrequently the case where there is not an established tradition of association with a particular school, William's younger brother Spencer and his sister Ellen went farther afield to school, in both cases to London.

The picture is very different for the farm workers and their children; for them, the village school, and in time the National School (often designated the British School), supported by subscriptions from the Freemans and others of their class. The school in the village was usually a church foundation, and the children attended the Sunday School and the church services often under the supervision of the schoolmaster.

Mrs Felgate went to the village school at Grundisburgh.

'The best toimes were the Sundays. I used to go to Sunday School in the mornin', from there to church; then go home to dinner. After dinner go back to Sunday School again, and then if that's a noice day, Mother 'd be riddy when I got home, we'd go for a walk till tea toime and then after tea, if that was foine, Mother and I'd go to Church. That's my Sunday.'

For Kenneth Stollery of Westleton, a Suffolk fishing village, Sunday was also a memorable day, but for other reasons:

'When we used to goo to Sunday School Mr. Gladwyn, the Schoolie, used to march us through the Vicarage grounds to Charch. to the eleven o'clock sarvice, and in the bard-nest'n' season, when we got to the east end corner, Gladwyn was at the hid of the column, y' see, and we used to run along at the back of the church, and stay at the west door till they were all in, and then we used to goo bard-nest'n'. During the day, he would count his flock, and find some missin', and on Monday mornin' he used to get back to *wark*! We had a little old song about that, we used to say:

> *Mr. Gladwyn is a very good man*
> *He goo to charch on Sunday*
> *And prays to God to give him strength*
> *To thrash the boys o' Monday.'*

Mrs Fosdyke, also of Westleton, recollected another custom, prevalent also in Essex: 'I can well remember when we used to go to school. On May 29th, Oak Apple Day, if we didn't have, or wear, an oak apple, you, and lots of other lads used to carry bunches of nettles, and sting us on the backs of our legs as much as ever you could.' This custom still survives at one of the public schools in Suffolk, though an oak apple is not obligatory; a leaf will do.

Charlie Hill was born at Iken, Suffolk, in 1892. On his thirteenth birthday, a Friday, he went to the schoolmaster, and apprised him of the fact, whereupon he was told, 'You may leave tonight.' The squire did not like to see the young idle, and all the stewards on his many farms were told to find employment for any lad as soon as he left school. So Charlie, as already mentioned, did not have to wait to find work. He was set on to help the cowman, at 3*s.* 6*d.* a week. From April to October, working hours were from 6.0 a.m. to 5.30 p.m.; from October to April, 7.0. to 5.0; Sundays, 7.0 a.m. to 9.30 a.m. Charlie, however, did not have to wait as long as most of his fellows to get a man's wage, for at the age of seventeen he was promoted to cowman in his own right. 'Y'see, the old man, he hung hisself!' The usual age for such promotion was twenty-one, 'and you wouldn't get a man's pay until you could carry a sack o' wheat and put it on the wagon. Well, I could play wi' it when I was seventeen.' So his wages rose from 3*s.* 6*d.* to 14*s.* at a bound. In due course he acquired a small farm of his own. He had no ambition to go far afield, and was very content with his lot. 'I've had a happy life,' he said when submitting to the ordeal by tape-recorder, echoing Mrs Felgate. 'They was 'appy toimes, 'appy toimes!'

Although there was a customary scale of wages, a separate agreement was negotiated with each individual, and the wage varied according to age and the duties required. Charles Freeman was careful to note in his diary each time he took on a man or servant. He almost invariably specified the time of appointment, so that when payment became due, there could be no dispute as to whether a day had been worked or not.

'1823. Oct. 19. John Doe came into house on Friday Oct. 17th to D. [dinner]. I am to give him 5£ for 50 weeks commencing from that day to do anything I like to set him after.'

John Doe's function was evidently that of *back'us boy.* Presumably he proved a good worker, for about a year later, promotion is mooted.

'1824. Sept. 1. Asked John Doe if he would like to see after my cart horses after Michaelmas and he is to consider of it a day or two and let me know, not a word mentioned about wages.'

'Oct. 11. Rachel Keeble came into my service for one Year at 6. 16. 6.'

Evidently an experienced servant, for:

'1824. Oct. 12. Mary Bollison of Burgate came into my service for 50 weeks to have the same as Susan Frost had 50/–.'

'1826. Oct. 13. Isaiah Garnham came into my service Oct. 12 *at night* to have 10/*s.* a month for 11 months and 50/– for a month in Harvest.'

'Oct. 15. Wm. Cooke belonging to Bedingfield came into my service at night to have 4£ for 50 weeks to do Man's work in Harvest.'

'1827. Oct. 13. Jonathan Hutton came into my service at night to have 2/s. per week and 2£ for 5 weeks in Harvest. If I keep him so long. to leave at a week's notice on receiving a week's pay. And Visa Versa.'

It would appear from the above examples that the custom of making a joint agreement with the full complement of workers on the farm was by-passed, or did not at that time apply.

Jonathan Hutton left after fourteen weeks; in stating the period of service when paying him his dues, both the day on which he came at *night*, Oct. 13th, and that on which he departed, presumably in the morning, January 19th, are given, although he is not of course paid for these days; fourteen weeks service at 2/– per week: £1. 8. 0.

In 1907 W. Rogers made the following agreement with an employee:

'Oct. 12th 1907. Hired D. Peck as Yard-Man at 13/– per week. House Rent Free, hours from Six A.M. to Six P.M. ½ hour at Breakfast one hour at dinner firewood within reason by cutting same. Subject to one Month Notice either side. W. S. Rogers. Hireing Money 1.0.'

Mrs Leonard, of Risby, near Bury St Edmunds, born in 1885, and of much the same generation as Mrs Felgate of Playford, had much the same experience so far as schooling and church-going were concerned. She went into service just before reaching the age of fourteen, receiving two shillings a week. She told of her work:

'Kitchen mornin's, I had to get up at foive—clean the kitchen flues, and so forth. Sunday if we got to bed afore quarter to ten, I was fortunate. It niver used to be much before ten o'clock. We had a half-day off Saturdays; we niver had no other day off . . . We always had to wear bonnets, to go to church with, and you niver dare cast your eyes on to anybody.'

Asked how she came to marry—'He used to be up there with my stepfather—and course, there you were . . . he'd come and go for a walk, and so forth, but we were courting for just on twelve years afore we were married', which came about when she was twenty-five. At the age of eighty-four she sang for the record the intricate words of 'The Barley Mow', and the ballads of 'The Spinster of Fifty-three' and 'The Sailor Boy', with only the occasional lapse.

For the major crafts, a formal system of apprenticeship was the rule. Edward Cooke Vincent was the son of a surgeon at Wells, Norfolk. He had no wish to follow his father's profession, so at the age of seventeen he was apprenticed to Amos Tiffen of Boxford, Suffolk, Miller and Maltster. The Indenture, was signed on 19th June 1861, but applied

'from the fourth day of April now last past unto the full End and Term of Four Years from thence next following to be fully complete and ended During which Term the said Apprentice his Master faithfully shall serve his secrets keep his lawful commands everywhere gladly shall he do he shall do no damage to his said Master of the same he shall not waste the Goods of his said Master nor lend them unlawfully to any he shall not commit fornication nor contract Matrimony within the said Term shall not play at Cards or Dice Tables or any other unlawful Games whereby his said Master may have any loss with his own goods or others during the said Term without Licence of his said Master shall neither buy nor sell he shall not haunt Taverns or Playhouses nor absent himself from his said Master's service day or night unlawfully But in all things as a faithful Apprentice he shall behave himself towards his said Master and all his during the said Term And the said Amos Tiffen in consideration of the sum of Thirty pounds sterling paid to him by the said Patrick Vincent upon the execution hereof the receipt whereof is hereby acknowledged And of the further sum of Thirty pounds to be paid as hereinafter mentioned doth surely for himself his heirs executors and administrators covenant and agree with the said Patrick Vincent and the said Apprentice That the said Amos Tiffen ... his said Apprentice in the Art of a Miller and Maltster which he useth by the best means that he can shall teach and Instruct or cause to be taught and instructed Finding unto the said Apprentice good and sufficient Meat Drink Tools and Lodging and all other Necessaries during the said Term And the said Patrick Vincent for himself his executors and administrators doth hereby covenant and agree with the said Amos Tiffen That he the said Patrick Vincent his executors and administrators will pay the said further sum of Thirty pounds to the said Amos Tiffen on the fourth day of April 1863 And also during the said term of four years find and provide for the said Apprentice sufficient and suitable clothes washing medicine and all other necessaries (except as aforesaid) And also that the said Apprentice shall well and faithfully serve his said Master in manner aforesaid.'

Small wonder that with all these limitations on the use of his leisure, Edward Vincent applied himself to the task of making a working model of the mill in which he worked, a model which may be seen, through the courtesy of his daughters, at the Abbot's Hall Museum. Soon after he completed it, the mill was burnt down.

The wives and children of farm workers, and the men themselves, were able from time to time to supplement regular wages by seasonal and part-time jobs. Such were planting the seeds following the dibblers, hoeing, singling beet, helping at harvest time, and stone-picking. This last was needed to supply the metalling for farm roads, and in some cases for use in the walls of buildings and those surrounding the yards.

Stone-picking is mentioned in the Freeman diaries for 1855, but much more detail is given in the account books of W. Rogers of Ilketshall St Margaret from 1897 onwards. F. Whatling and Burrows Junr. received respectively 1s. 4d. for 16 bushels of stones and 5s. 10d. for 70 bushels—1d. per bushel; in 1899, R. Saxby picked 148 bushels, and received 18s. 6d., at the rate of 1½d., and the same rate is paid to one Page in 1902. The champion of them all seems to have been Polly Whatling, probably the mother of F. Whatling noted above. In April 1905 she picked 85 bushels at 1½d., and her name recurs frequently. If she is not stone-picking, she is singling beet or turnips. Boy Catling received £1. 16. 0 for 12 loads, so it would appear that 24 bushels constituted a load. The main purpose was for making up the roads, but a Suffolk farmer, noted for his experiments in matters agricultural, set out to test the merits or otherwise of stone-picking in relation to cropping. His results are recorded by Thomas Potts (1808):

'Mr. Macro of Suffolk, having often suspected, that removing stones from turnip land did more hurt than good, resolved to convince himself by experiment whether he were right or not: he therefore gathered up all the stones of one square rod, after the turnips were folded off, and laid them equally over another square by the side of it, then sowed them with barley, and marked them out, and at harvest time, collected them separately, as likewise another square rod by the side of them, which had only the natural quantity of stones.

	Coombs	B.	P.
Produce from the rod that had the double quantity of stones			
6 quarts, 1 pint, or per acre	8	0	0
Do. from that where the stones were gathered off			
6 do.	7	2	0
D. from that in its natural state			
6 do.	7	3	1

From this single experiment, the result is in favour of the largest quantity of stones.'

Anyone who has attempted to get rid of the stones in Suffolk soil will realize that Nature has provided a bottomless reservoir for their replenishment year by year.

A payment unvarying over the years was that for mole-catching, at 15s. 0d. for the year. This was not, however, something to be left to one of the local boys, but needed a special skill. The mole-catcher in the Ilketshall district was, appropriately, John Hunting, who flourished in the early years of the century. His counterpart in mid Suffolk was known as 'Slapper' Rice, and his son who succeeded him in the task adopted the same pseudonym.

Just as work is regulated by the nature of the surroundings, so with play. Suffolk, and the rural area of Essex, consist of gently undulating country, largely given over to agriculture, with a coastline of low cliffs or dunes, intersected by the mouths of rivers. For those able to afford them, therefore, ideal conditions exist for the three traditional English forms of sport, hunting, shooting and fishing, and a fourth with almost as large a following where it is practicable—sailing.

Foxhounds seem usually to have been privately owned, though Brig. General C. D. Bruce, writing in 1926, records that the pack formed by Harding Newman of Nelmes near Romford in 1785 came to be known by 1795 as 'the Essex Subscription Foxhounds'. From 1808 to 1813 Colonel John Cook, a renowned Essex sportsman, was Master of the Essex Hunt.

Charles Freeman was a dedicated rider to hounds, whether it was the fox or the stag which was the quarry. His diary for the spring of 1827 gives detailed accounts of his sallies with fox-hounds, harriers and stag-hounds. He was out at least twice a week, ending up with a stag run on 6th April, and a doe with the Union Harriers at Whitton on the 7th 'came home as wet as a Water Dog'.

The clergy found in blood sports nothing inconsistent with their calling. An Essex parson, asked if he ever thought of anything but hunting, replied, 'I never think of *hunting* until after Morning Service'.

William Freeman seems to have been less keen on active hunting than his father. He enjoyed race meetings, attending the steeplechases at Diss in Norfolk, and at Newmarket, where he went on 22nd April 1851 to see the 2,000 guineas stakes. 'Won 3 shillings of Walter Birch, he backing the field against the Favorites'.

William's great love was the sea, and he took every opportunity to accompany his great friend—and later brother-in-law—Owen Ridley of Ipswich, in the latter's boat *Swallow*, sailing frequently from Ipswich to Harwich. On one such occasion they were caught in a squall in Harwich harbour and had to down sail. They made the best of things however by pulling over to Landguard Fort, where they took wine and biscuits with one of the Militia officers. On the return trip they shipped half a boat full of water, and had to spend the night with Owen's sister at Holbrook, having to 'pull' (row) to Ipswich 'a distance of 20 miles against wind and tide, arriving at midnight'.

The chance to visit Royal Ascot took precedence even over sailing, and received the further reward of seeing 'all the Royal Family who drove on the course with eleven carriages with four horses each'.

Shooting was largely a private occasion; it is only comparatively recently that the renting of shooting rights to syndicates has become the rule rather than the exception, for economic reasons.

Many Suffolk houses are moated, and this made skating a popular pastime. William Freeman skated whenever opportunity occurred on the moat and ponds at Stowupland Hall, and also went frequently to Abbot's Hall in the centre of Stowmarket, then unoccupied. He writes of skating on the 'moat' there, but this was in fact the main ornamental pond, one of four which have existed since the fifteenth century, and were the fishponds of the grange of the Abbots of St Osyth, to which foundation the whole of the Stowmarket area had been granted by Henry II.

The small green outside the wall encircling the grounds of Abbot's Hall, and possibly a part of the enclosed area, made up the 'Camping Land', where the game of camp, traditional to Suffolk, was played; it was also known in Essex and possibly in Norfolk too. The term 'Camping pightel' occurs in a deed of 1486. Thomas Tusser, quoted by Moor (1823), regarded the treading down of the meadow involved as of benefit to the ground:

> *'In meadow or pasture—(to grow the more fine)*
> *Let campers be camping in any of thine:*
> *Which if ye do suffer when low is the spring,*
> *You gain to yourself a commodious thing.'*

and—

> *'Get campers a ball, To camp therewithall.'*

Both Moor and Claxton (1968) give a very full description of it; space does not permit a full account here. It seems to have had something in common with Rugby football, or the Eton Wall Game, and could certainly be dangerous; report says that two men were killed at a game at Easton about 1870, and it then fell into disfavour. Originally it was played with a ball about the size of a cricket ball, though later a football seems to have been used. The holder of the ball had 'if caught and held, or in imminent danger of being caught' to throw the ball 'to a lesser beleaguered friend'. If caught with the ball actually in his possession, he lost a 'snotch'. 'Seven or nine snotches are the game—and these will sometimes take two or three hours to win.' The game was played by schools, and also by parish teams.

Another purely local game was three-pin bowling, traditionally associated with the Goose Fair and similar events. The three 'pins' (skittles) were set up at points determined by means of a heavy iron triangle, spiked to hold it in place; the 'wood' resembled that used in the game of bowls but was smaller, and bound with a broad iron band.

For the game of quoits, a bed of clay was laid down as a target; the quoits, made by the blacksmith, varied in size, but the average for men weighed three pounds. Village competed with village, and many a turn must have been played outside the local, but when winter came, and the light faded, the ranks of the regulars inside would be swelled by the darts team from a neighbouring parish. The Suffolk darts board differs, or did, from the regular pattern in the arrangement of the numbers.

Some few years ago, when the Beccles White Lion changed hands, and use, it was found to have a cock-fighting floor, made from small pebbles about the size of a bantam's egg, to give a grip for the claws of the combatants. Regrettably, a suggestion that it be removed to an appropriate museum was ignored by the new owners, and so the material relic of an ancient pastime was lost to posterity.

No account of the daily life of the community would be complete without some reference to religion in its various forms. Space will not permit a detailed survey, and our concern will therefore be rather on its impact on local relationships; the monuments which it has left behind are discussed in another chapter. It was responsible for many notable buildings—parish churches and monastic foundations, and some satisfying examples of architecture amongst the non-conformist groups, as for example the Unitarian chapels at Bury St Edmunds and Ipswich. But it brought other less desirable manifestations; major dissensions which led to persecution and martyrdom, and to the despoiling of many priceless treasures in our churches; lesser disagreements caused by the dislike of the non-conformists amongst the farming community of the obligation to pay tithes to the representatives of the Established Church.

Thomas Tusser was one of those who paid their tithes without demur, and he conjured others to follow suit:

'Pay justly thy tithes, whatever thou be,
that God may in blessing, send foison to thee:
Though curate be bad, or the parson as evil,
go not for thy tithing, thyself to the devil.'

In Tusser's time, and for centuries later, tithes were by custom paid in kind. A Tithe Commutation Act, substituting a cash payment, was passed in 1836, but some farmers evidently made a practice of compounding voluntarily, by arrangement with the incumbent. One of these was Charles Freeman, of Stowupland Hall, as the following entries in his diary show:

'1822. August 8. Mr. Wm. Aldridge
　　　　　　Vicarial Tythe　　　　　　　9. 6. 0.
　1823. August 6. Mr. Aldrich* and son came and dined with me.
　　　　Agreed with Mr. Aldrich to pay 6. 10. 6. for small Tithe for 14 years for
　　　　me to pay all Rates and Charges.'

and in his accounts:

　'Per Mr. Aldrich Tithe due at Lammas day. he took off 30 per cent from
　£9. 6. 0. which I used to pay and I allowed 35/s, for 3 Years Rates he paid.
　paid him　　　　　　　　　　　7. 15. 0.
　1824. Pd. Mr. Aldridge Tithe　　　　6. 10. 6.
　　　　not a word said about Easter Offerings by either party.
　　　　I did not pay any at Easter.'

There is no mention of any tithe payment in 1827, although he paid his pew rent of £3. 5. 0., but he paid again in 1828, when he also made an arrangement in respect of land in the parish of Earl Stonham:

'Agreed with Mr. Phear* of Earl Stonham to pay £2. 10. 0. a year as composition for Tithes for as long a time as both parties live. Mr. Phear said he had to take Tithe on Nine Acres of land. I told him I could not set the Tithe out if we could not agree.'

An even earlier case of the voluntary payment of a tithe is quoted by Joan Thirsk and Jean Imray (1958), culled from the *Carter Family Papers* in the Suffolk Record Office at Bury St Edmunds:

'Jany. 1, 1806.
'I Henry Carter having this day compleated the forty-eight year of my aage and the Lord haveing prospered my endavours and blessed the work of my hands and increased my worldly substance beyond my utmost expectations I do from this time forward dedycate the tenth part of the increase thereof to religious and charytable

* His spelling was arbitrary, and varied from year to year. Wm. Aldrich was the Vicar of Stowmarket, John Phear the rector of Earl Stonham.

purposes and I intend keeping a book of my distributions and to balance it with the increase at the end of each year on this paper and my desire is that my executors or whosoever may have the management of my affairs after my decease may faithfully apply it to the use for which it is intended. Relying on divine grace to make me faithfull to this my ingagement and trusting in His good providence to succeed my indavours knowing that I am a sinfull creature and can merit nothing at the hands of my Creater I pray for mercy and pardon through the merits and riteousness of Jesus Christ.'

But it was equally devout Christians who resented the imposition of tithes. Philip Butler, farmer, artist and poet, and at the time a member of the Society of Friends, suffered the seizure of his stock for the recovery of unpaid tithes. A sale was held, and he has recorded the scene in oils, depicting the disposition of the final lot, a piglet—the proceeds to go to charity. A number of local stalwarts of the anti-tithe movement may be recognized, Messrs A. G. Mobbs and Rowley Rash, and the founder of the movement for the use of purely organic media in the cultivation of food crops, Lady Eve Balfour; the painting may be seen at the Abbot's Hall Museum.

Belief in the supernatural did not manifest itself solely in the practice of organized religion. The countryside, even perhaps more than the town, was a fertile breeding ground for the growth of superstition. Witchcraft flourished in the region, and the two counties are linked in having provided the field for the activities of the notorious Matthew Hopkins, self-styled 'Witchfinder Generall', who was responsible for the deaths of some hundreds of innocent victims. The son of a Suffolk minister, he studied the law, and failing to make a livelihood at this profession in Ipswich, he moved to Manningtree, from where he began his nefarious work. Relics of the deeply-rooted belief in the power of witches are still to be found, not infrequently, in the discovery of 'witch-bottles'—stoneware Bellarmine jars, buried under the hearth or threshold of a cottage. Some account of the first known example of this practice is to be found in Joseph Glanvil's *Sadducismus Triumphatus*, or full and plain Evidence concerning Witches and Apparitions, published in 1681, and details of recent finds in Suffolk have been published in the *Proceedings of the Suffolk Institute of Archaeology* from time to time.* Evidences of the revival of the practice of black magic have been found in a number of Suffolk churchyards in recent years.

* In particular, 'More Suffolk Witch-bottles', by Norman Smedley and Elizabeth Owles, *Proceedings of the Suffolk Institute of Archeology*, vol. XXX, Part 1 (1964).

Works Cited

British Farmers Cyclopaedia, The, 1808.

BAGSHAWE, T., 1956. *Rake and Scythe-Handle making in Bedfordshire and Suffolk* (in *Gwerin*, Vol. I, No. 2).

BROWN, A. F. J., 1969. *Essex at Work 1700–1815*.

BRUNSKILL, R. W., 1971. *Illustrated Handbook of Vernacular Architecture*.

CAMDEN, W., 1607 edn. *Britannia*.

CLAXTON, A. O. D., 1968. *The Suffolk Dialect of the Twentieth Century*, 3rd edn.

COBBETT, W., 1829. *Rural Rides*.

Country Gentleman's Catalogue, 1894.

COPELAND, J., 1968. *Roads and their Traffic*.

EVANS, G. E., 1970. *Where Beards Wag All*.

FITZHERBERT, J., 1523. *Booke of Husbandrie*.

GLANVIL, JOSEPH, 1681. *Sadducismus Triumphatus*

JENKINS, J. G., 1965. *Traditional Country Craftsmen*.

JOBSON, A., 1953. *Household and Country Crafts*.

KETTERIDGE, C., and MAYS, S., 1972. *Five Miles from Bunkum*.

KIRBY, J., 1744. *Suffolk Traveller*, 2nd edn.

MARSHALL, W., 1795. *Rural Economy of Norfolk*, 2nd edn.

MOOR, E., 1823. *Suffolk Words and Phrases*.

MORTON, J. C., 1855. *A Cyclopaedia of Agriculture*.

NARES, R., 1822. *Classical Glossary*.

POTTS, T., 1808. *A Cyclopaedia of Agriculture*, 2nd edn.

PROTHERO, R. E., 1917. *English Farming Past and Present*.

RANSOME, J. A., 1843. *The Implements of Agriculture*.

RAY, J., 1768. *English Proverbs*.

RAYNBIRD, W. and H., 1849. *On the Agriculture of Suffolk*.

SCARFE, N., 1960. *Suffolk: a Shell Guide*; 1968. *Essex: a Shell Guide*.

SMITH, J. T., 1958. *A 14th Century Aisled House: Edgar's Farm, Stowmarket* (in Proc. Suff. Inst. Arch., Vol. XXVIII).

SPENCER, H. E. P., 1966–7 and 1970–2. *A Contribution to the Geological History of Suffolk* (in Trans. Suff. Nat. Soc.).

STEPHENS, H., 1888. *Book of the Farm* (4th edn.).

THIRSK, J., and IMRAY, J., 1958. *Suffolk Farming in the Nineteenth Century.* Suffolk Records Society, Vol. I.

TRIST, P. J. O., 1971. *A Survey of the Agriculture of Suffolk.*

TUSSER, T., 1557. *A hundred good poyntes of husbandry.*

White's Directory of Suffolk, 1844.

WRIGHT, P., 1961. *Old Farm Implements.*

YOUNG, A., 1771. *A Farmer's Tour Through the East of England*; 1797 and 1813. *A General View of the Agriculture of Suffolk*; 1807. *Report on the Agriculture of Essex.*

Index

meaning a circumference = traveller 28

compass 27